SpringerBriefs in Computer Science

SpringerBriefs present concise summaries of cutting-edge research and practical applications across a wide spectrum of fields. Featuring compact volumes of 50 to 125 pages, the series covers a range of content from professional to academic.

Typical topics might include:

- A timely report of state-of-the art analytical techniques
- A bridge between new research results, as published in journal articles, and a contextual literature review
- A snapshot of a hot or emerging topic
- An in-depth case study or clinical example
- A presentation of core concepts that students must understand in order to make independent contributions

Briefs allow authors to present their ideas and readers to absorb them with minimal time investment. Briefs will be published as part of Springer's eBook collection, with millions of users worldwide. In addition, Briefs will be available for individual print and electronic purchase. Briefs are characterized by fast, global electronic dissemination, standard publishing contracts, easy-to-use manuscript preparation and formatting guidelines, and expedited production schedules. We aim for publication 8–12 weeks after acceptance. Both solicited and unsolicited manuscripts are considered for publication in this series.

**Indexing: This series is indexed in Scopus, Ei-Compendex, and zbMATH **

Tao Zhang • Xiangyun Tang • Jiawen Kang • Changqiao Xu

Moving Target Defense Based on Artificial Intelligence

Tao Zhang
School of Cyberspace Science and Technology
Beijing Jiaotong University
Beijing, China

Jiawen Kang
School of Automation
Guangdong University of Technology
Guangzhou, Guangdong, China

Xiangyun Tang
School of Information Engineering
Minzu University of China
Beijing, China

Changqiao Xu
School of Computer Science
Beijing University of Posts and Telecommunications
Beijing, China

ISSN 2191-5768   ISSN 2191-5776   (electronic)
SpringerBriefs in Computer Science
ISBN 978-981-95-0614-9   ISBN 978-981-95-0615-6   (eBook)
https://doi.org/10.1007/978-981-95-0615-6

© The Editor(s) (if applicable) and The Author(s), under exclusive license to Springer Nature Singapore Pte Ltd. 2026

This work is subject to copyright. All rights are solely and exclusively licensed by the Publisher, whether the whole or part of the material is concerned, specifically the rights of translation, reprinting, reuse of illustrations, recitation, broadcasting, reproduction on microfilms or in any other physical way, and transmission or information storage and retrieval, electronic adaptation, computer software, or by similar or dissimilar methodology now known or hereafter developed.
The use of general descriptive names, registered names, trademarks, service marks, etc. in this publication does not imply, even in the absence of a specific statement, that such names are exempt from the relevant protective laws and regulations and therefore free for general use.
The publisher, the authors and the editors are safe to assume that the advice and information in this book are believed to be true and accurate at the date of publication. Neither the publisher nor the authors or the editors give a warranty, expressed or implied, with respect to the material contained herein or for any errors or omissions that may have been made. The publisher remains neutral with regard to jurisdictional claims in published maps and institutional affiliations.

This Springer imprint is published by the registered company Springer Nature Singapore Pte Ltd.
The registered company address is: 152 Beach Road, #21-01/04 Gateway East, Singapore 189721, Singapore

If disposing of this product, please recycle the paper.

Preface

In the current age of increasingly advanced and rapidly changing attack techniques, attackers use various advanced cyberattack techniques to continuously challenge the existing defense system. Traditional defense mechanisms rely too heavily on the patterns and characteristics of known attacks, making it difficult to adequately safeguard the security of network systems. Moving Target Defense (MTD), a new defense paradigm, effectively defends against attacks through proactive defense strategies. Its core concept is unpredictability, which makes it difficult for attackers to plan and execute attacks. MTD disrupts the attacker's reconnaissance plan by constantly changing the attack surface, such as adjusting system configurations, network architectures, and other key components, greatly reducing the likelihood of a successful attack, while enhancing the system's ability to withstand unknown threats, providing a solid framework for dynamic security.

This book focuses on MTD defense approaches in cloud-edge-terminal network architectures. We propose intelligent MTD solutions for different network scenarios, with a special emphasis on the introduction of artificial intelligence (AI) techniques. By incorporating AI technologies, we aim to enhance the intelligence and adaptability of MTD approaches under different network conditions. AI empowers MTDs to learn during attacks, predictively analyze attack behaviors, and defend dynamically, thus ensuring a higher level of defense performance.

We believe that this book will be an indispensable resource for researchers and engineers working on intelligent MTD defense techniques. Whether you are a student just entering the field or a professional and researcher looking to deepen your understanding or implementation of MTD solutions, this book will provide invaluable guidance. By combining fundamental concepts with advanced methodologies, this book hopes to contribute to the advancement of MTD defense technology.

Beijing, China Tao Zhang
Beijing, China Xiangyun Tang
Guangzhou, Guangdong, China Jiawen Kang
Beijing, China Changqiao Xu

Acknowledgments

In writing this book on intelligent moving target defense, I have gone through a process that has been both challenging and rewarding, all of which could not have been achieved without the support and guidance of many people.

At the beginning, I would like to extend my heartfelt thanks to Prof. Dusit Niyato (Nanyang Technological University), Prof. Xiangyun Tang (Minzu University of China), Prof. Jiawen Kang (Guangdong University of Technology), and Prof. Changqiao Xu (Beijing University of Posts and Telecommunications). Their careful guidance and insightful feedback played an integral role in the writing of this book. Their expertise and encouragement continued to inspire me to explore new perspectives and overcome various obstacles in the writing process.

Second, I am deeply indebted to my colleagues, especially Jiqiang Liu, Xiaoqiang Zhu, and Jiacheng Wang, whose constructive discussions, technical insights, and valuable suggestions have greatly enriched this book. In addition, I would like to thank my students and research group members, including Shuang Tian, Tianhao Liu, Xuzeng Li, Wei Chen, and Longyu Li, whose curiosity and dedication provided a strong driving force for the many ideas and experiments in this special issue. Their enthusiasm and efforts have been a constant source of motivation for me to complete this book.

I would also like to thank the editorial team of Springer Nature for their professionalism and guidance, which helped make this book possible.

Finally, I would like to express my sincere gratitude to all those who have supported me directly or indirectly. The completion of this book is both a reflection of my personal efforts and a culmination of the combined efforts of many contributors.

Part of the work of this special issue was supported by the following grants, which are gratefully acknowledged: the National Cryptologic Science Fund of China under Grant 2025NCSF02030; the National Natural Science Foundation of China (NSFC) under Grants 62402029, 62302539; and the China Postdoctoral Science Foundation under Grant 2024T170047, Grant GZC20230223, and Grant 2024M750165.

Contents

1 **Introduction** 1
   1.1 Background 1
   1.2 Security Issues in Cloud-Edge-Terminal Network 3
       1.2.1 Security Threats to the Cloud Layer 4
       1.2.2 Security Threats to the Edge Layer 5
       1.2.3 Security Threats to the Terminal Layer 5
   1.3 Overview of Network-Based Moving Target Defense 6
       1.3.1 Design Principles 6
       1.3.2 Methods Classification 7
   1.4 Organization of the Book 9
   References 10

2 **AI-Driven Moving Target Defense: Host Address Mutation Based on Advantage Actor-Critic Approach** 13
   2.1 Introduction 13
       2.1.1 Motivations 13
       2.1.2 Challenges 14
       2.1.3 Contributions 14
       2.1.4 Related Work 15
   2.2 Model Formulation on the Cloud Layer 16
       2.2.1 Threat Model 16
       2.2.2 Network Model 17
       2.2.3 Markov Decision Process Model 18
   2.3 Detailed Design 20
       2.3.1 Address Allocation Formalization 20
       2.3.2 Intelligent Host Address Mutation 23
   2.4 Performance Evaluation and Analysis 26
       2.4.1 Defense Performance 26
       2.4.2 Convergence Performance 30
       2.4.3 Network Performance 31

2.5 Conclusion 33
References 33

3 AI-Driven Moving Target Defense for DTMN: Collaborative Mutation-Based Moving Target Defense Based on Hierarchical Reinforcement Learning 37
3.1 Introduction 37
    3.1.1 Motivations 37
    3.1.2 Challenges 38
    3.1.3 Contributions 38
    3.1.4 Related Work 40
3.2 Model Formulation on the Edge Layer 40
    3.2.1 Network Model 41
    3.2.2 Threat Model 41
    3.2.3 Semi-Markov Decision Process Model 42
3.3 Detailed Design 44
    3.3.1 Collaborative Mutation Formalization 45
    3.3.2 Intelligent Collaborative Mutation Scheme 47
3.4 Performance Evaluation and Analysis 50
    3.4.1 Prediction Performance 51
    3.4.2 Defense Performance 53
    3.4.3 Network Performance 55
3.5 Conclusion 56
References 56

4 AI-Driven Moving Target Defense Framework for SD-IoV: Roadside Unit Mutation via Proximal Policy Optimization 59
4.1 Introduction 59
    4.1.1 Motivations 59
    4.1.2 Challenges 60
    4.1.3 Contributions 61
    4.1.4 Related Work 61
4.2 Model Formulation on the Edge Layer 63
    4.2.1 Network Model 63
    4.2.2 Threat Model 64
4.3 Detailed Design 64
    4.3.1 Intelligent Mutation Mechanism 66
    4.3.2 Trust Assessment Mechanism 68
4.4 Performance Evaluation and Analysis 72
    4.4.1 Defense Performance 74
    4.4.2 Trustworthiness Performance 75
    4.4.3 Network Performance 76
4.5 Conclusion 77
References 77

5 AI-Driven Moving Target Defense for VANETs: Route Mutation via Multiagent Reinforcement Learning ... 81
5.1 Introduction ... 81
5.1.1 Motivations ... 81
5.1.2 Challenges ... 82
5.1.3 Related Work ... 84
5.2 Model Formulation on the End Layer ... 85
5.2.1 Network Model ... 85
5.2.2 Threat Model ... 86
5.2.3 Markov Decision Process Model ... 86
5.3 Detailed Design ... 89
5.3.1 Secure Grid Selection Based on Extended Joint Action Learning ... 90
5.3.2 Node Selection Strategy Inside Secure Grid ... 95
5.4 Performance Evaluation and Analysis ... 97
5.4.1 Defense Performance ... 99
5.4.2 Network Performance ... 100
5.5 Conclusion ... 103
References ... 103

6 Conclusion ... 107
6.1 Summary of the Book ... 107
6.2 Future Directions ... 109

Chapter 1
Introduction

Abstract With its dispersed and dynamic features, the cloud-edge-terminal network architecture offers customers effective and adaptable network services, satisfying the increasing demand for network services. However, this architecture also introduces additional security risks. This chapter will provide a comprehensive overview of the cloud-edge-terminal network architecture, briefly outline the specific components and network services provided by each layer, and conduct a thorough analysis of the network risks faced by each layer. Additionally, this chapter will explore Mobile Target Defence (MTD) technology, a novel defence technique employing proactive defence strategies, whose emergence offers a feasible technical approach for providing reliable security protection for cloud-edge-terminal networks. We will outline the fundamental design principles of MTD and, from the perspective of network operation mechanisms, classify mainstream MTD solutions into active virtual migration, proxy shuffling, and network property mutation. We will provide a detailed introduction to the defence principles of these three MTD solutions and list specific system cases. This chapter provides the background information readers need to comprehend the book's content by introducing cloud-edge-terminal networks and MTD technology.

Keywords Moving target defense · Artificial intelligence · Cloud-edge-terminal network · Artificial intelligence-driven network · Security analysis

1.1 Background

The number and complexity of network devices are growing exponentially due to the quick advancement of technology and the ongoing rise in network demand [1]. The advancement of the digitalization process has also increased the complexity of the network structure [2, 3]. These changes not only expand the network attack surface, but also provide new soil for the development of attack techniques. Advances in cyberattack technology have dramatically increased the frequency, stealth, and unpredictability of attacks, increasing the threat of attacks and the difficulty of protecting current networks [4]. Cloud-edge-terminal architecture is a widely used and important network architecture at present [5], and its distributed and dynamic characteristics, although providing great advantages for the efficiency and flexibility of network services, also expose more security risks. The centralized nature of cloud resources makes them a key target for attackers. The large number and high diversity of edge devices, and the security differences between the devices further exacerbate the vulnerability of the overall system. The terminal devices, due to their direct interaction with the user, often become the main target for attackers to take advantage of the vulnerability of user behavior to carry out attacks. Therefore, the cloud-edge-end network architecture significantly expands the potential attack surface and threat dimension while enhancing network performance. In 2024, Telecommunications company AT&T is attacked in which hackers use insecure storage accounts on a cloud-based service to steal customer data, and the company ultimately pays the hacking group approximately $370,000 in cryptocurrency to ensure that the stolen data was deleted from public view. In the above case, the attacker successfully breached the protective barrier posed by traditional techniques through advanced attack techniques and caused huge economic losses. This clearly illustrates how the conventional network protection techniques, which are based on the concept of passive defense, have gradually demonstrated their performance shortcomings and are unable to offer adequate security in the current highly dynamic and distributed network environment in the face of such complex and evolving threats [6].

The MTD defense scheme, which adopts the idea of proactive defense, provides a feasible technical path to improve the network defense performance in the cloud-edge-terminal networks. MTD weakens an attacker's intrinsic detection advantage over a network system and raises the complexity and time cost of attacks by continuously switching between several network system configurations, such as altering open network ports, network settings, and software. This novel idea of adversarial defense provides a new technical path for future network defense, but it also provides additional technical difficulties for its implementation and practical deployment [7]. But the emergence of Network Functions Virtualization (NFV) and Software-Defined Networking (SDN) provides a feasible low-cost solution for MTD. NFV allows flexible deployment and dynamic adjustment of network functions by virtualizing the functions of traditional hardware network devices into software forms, which allows the frequent changes in network configuration required for MTD to be easily achieved in a virtualized environment. By divorcing the network control plane from the data plane, SDN offers a centralized method of network management. With SDN, MTD can flexibly allocate network resources, adjust network topology, and dynamically manage communication paths to realize flexible changes in network configuration. On the other hand, MTD technology is also highly scalable and can utilize technologies such as big data and artificial intelligence to further enhance its defense capabilities, increase the randomness of MTD technology's defense mobility strategy and reduce its defense costs. At the same time, it can also be combined with blockchain, edge technology and other technologies to effectively expand its application scenarios and enhance the versatility of MTD technology.

This book focuses on MTD applications in cloud-edge-terminal network scenarios. In the next part of this chapter, we will briefly introduce cloud-edge-terminal networks and analyze the major cyber threats they face (will be discussed in detail in Sect. 1.2). Subsequently, we will explore the concepts related to network-based MTD and analyze the ways in which current MTD schemes are applied in network defense (will be discussed in detail in Sect. 1.3). Finally, we will briefly introduce the overall structure of the remaining chapters of the book (will be discussed in detail in Sect. 1.4).

1.2 Security Issues in Cloud-Edge-Terminal Network

As edge computing gains popularity, cloud-edge-terminal networks are becoming a prominent and widely-used network architecture. The AI-driven network architecture integrates the cloud's processing power, edge computing's responsiveness, and terminal devices' intelligent interaction to enable efficient collaboration and smart application of resources. Through distributed collaboration and layered processing, the network enables AI tasks to run efficiently and drives a shift in computing paradigm from centralized clouds to flexible distributed architectures. In the cloud layer, the network accomplishes the processing of complex tasks through centralized high-performance computing and huge storage resources. The cloud is suitable for running deep learning model training and big data mining tasks, such as model training for natural language processing, large-scale image analysis, and model development based on multimodal data. The cloud also supports, for example, distributed database management and efficient scientific simulation tasks. In order to deliver low-latency and high-real-time computing services for tasks with dynamic contexts, the network employs nodes near the data source at the edge layer. Edge nodes can run edge-optimized algorithms such as deep neural networks for real-time traffic flow analysis, adaptive filters for preprocessing sensor data, and personalized recommendation algorithms based on local data. The edge layer also supports fast decision-making and anomaly detection tasks in industrial automation. At the terminal layer, the network enables localized data processing and real-time response through direct interaction with the user's device. Terminal devices can run lightweight machine learning algorithms, such as speech recognition models to support intelligent voice assistants, enhanced reality applications based on image classification, and personalized health data analytics through on-device reasoning. The terminal layer is also capable of combining resources at the edge and the cloud to provide users with high-quality interactive experiences, such as real-time translation, smart home control, and mobile payment security.

However, along with the many conveniences that cloud-edge-terminal network offers, it also faces numerous security issues, which we will address in detail in the remaining three subsections of this subsection.

1.2.1 Security Threats to the Cloud Layer

The cloud layer is central to the cloud-edge-terminal architecture, offering diverse cloud computing services. These services can be broadly categorized into three types: infrastructure as a service (IaaS), platform as a service (PaaS), and software as a service (SaaS). IaaS, the foundation of cloud computing, gives customers access to virtualized computer resources including networking, storage, and virtual machines. Users can allocate resources based on demand without acquiring and maintaining physical hardware [8]. This flexible and low-cost service mode has become the preferred choice of many enterprises and developers. PaaS builds on the IaaS to provide a unified platform for developing and deploying applications. By abstracting the underlying infrastructure, it reduces the complexity of application development and frees developers to concentrate on feature design and coding. SaaS is the top tier of cloud computing services, delivering software applications directly to end users. It typically relies on PaaS and IaaS for support. This mode allows users to access applications over the Internet without installing and maintaining software [9], thus lowering the barrier to use and cost of ownership.

However, while the cloud provides powerful computing capabilities, it also faces many security threats. The main threats include malicious network reconnaissance, DDoS attacks, co-residence and side-channel attacks. The homogenized infrastructure shared in multi-tenant cloud environments makes it easier for attackers to perform scans and locate their targets, a characteristic that is especially noticeable in IaaS environments [10]. Attackers can scan the virtualized network of a cloud environment to discover vulnerabilities or exploitable resources. Moreover, such attacks are often difficult to detect. Common methods of attack include identifying open ports using port scanning techniques, speculating on network architecture through traffic analysis, and exploiting API vulnerabilities for data leakage. The shared and scalable nature of cloud resources provides convenient conditions for DDoS attacks. Through many queries, the attacker uses up the target system's processing, storage, and network bandwidth resources, paralyzing or even stopping regular services entirely. Bandwidth depletion and resource depletion attacks are two common ways of DDoS attacks. The attacker fills up the network bandwidth or depletes the resources of the target system through a large number of forged requests, thus affecting the normal services or paralyzing the entire system. In cloud environments, these attacks are usually launched jointly through botnets and utilize the elastic scaling mechanism of cloud platforms to exacerbate the impact, not only degrading service performance but also significantly increasing operational costs. Co-residence and side-channel attacks are also important threats in the cloud. These types of attacks steal sensitive data by exploiting shared resources such as processor caches, memory, or virtual machine hosts between different tenants in a multi-tenant environment. Attackers can gain access to keys, passwords, or other private information through side-channel analysis, thus posing a serious security risk to the target system.

1.2.2 Security Threats to the Edge Layer

The edge layer of the cloud-edge-terminal network, which acts as a bridge between the terminal and cloud layers, is in charge of processing, managing, and storing the data that is gathered from the terminal layer as well as filtering and integrating the data that is uploaded to the cloud. In addition to improving data quality and lessening the cloud layer's computational and storage strain, this architecture also decreases data transmission latency and uploads less redundant data.

The edge layer consists of three key components: edge controller, edge server and edge gateway. The edge controller is the coordinator of the edge layer, undertaking task allocation and resource management, and guaranteeing communication and control between edge layer devices. The edge server focuses on data processing and storage, covering data modeling, aggregation processing, and operational control to support heterogeneous computing, providing support for efficient data analysis and cloud-edge collaboration. The edge gateway, on the other hand, focuses on device management and data flow, and is responsible for device registration, data caching, and optimizing the data processing process using edge intelligence. These three synergies together support the efficient operation of the edge layer.

Resource depletion attacks, particularly DDoS attacks, are more likely to target edge layer nodes because of their low resources. This attack affects the normal services provided by the nodes in the edge layer by sending the many requests to the nodes to exhaust their resources [11]. Common types of edge layer DDoS attacks include Smurf attacks, SYN Flood attacks and UDP Flood attacks. Attackers using UDP Flood attack edge nodes with forged UDP packets, causing them to become overloaded with processing erroneous requests and unable to reply to authentic traffic. The SYN Flood attack utilizes the three handshakes in the TCP protocol to tie up the connection queue resources of the edge server by spoofing a large number of outstanding connection requests. The Smurf attack floods the target by sending forged ICMP requests to broadcast addresses, spoofing the target's address as the source.

1.2.3 Security Threats to the Terminal Layer

The terminal layer is a collection of devices directly facing the user, including Internet of Things (IoT) devices, smartphones, and sensors. It is responsible for data collection, initial processing and communication with the edge or cloud layer. Devices in the terminal layer perform data collection work and then upload it to the edge or cloud layer after local preliminary processing, and the terminal devices will then perform corresponding operations based on the returned analyzed decision results.

However, the importance and openness of this layer also makes it a prime target for cybersecurity threats. Since wireless networks play an important part in connecting the terminal layer to the edge or cloud layer, these connections are typically more vulnerable to man-in-the-middle attacks or black hole attacks. An attacker manipulates or hijacks a communication link to tamper with or drop packets on the link to achieve illegal control or disruption [12]. An attacker can use a man-in-the-middle attack to intercept and decrypt data sent at the terminal layer by pretending to be a genuine network node or access point and then injecting malicious data to control devices or steal confidential data. A black hole attack refers to an attacker controlling a node in the network to make it a "black hole" for data, intercepting and discarding all packets passing through the node, thus affecting the normal network function [13].

1.3 Overview of Network-Based Moving Target Defense

According to Manadhata et al. [14], the term "attack surface" refers to the collection of potential entryways for an attacker into a system. Based on this concept, MTD was proposed by the Networking and Information Technology Research and Development program [15]. Then, MTD was divided into five categories by Okhravi et al. [16], including dynamic network, dynamic platform, dynamic execution environment, dynamic software, and dynamic data. In this book, we focus on dynamic network, which are considered as network-based MTD.

1.3.1 Design Principles

Three questions will form the foundation of the MTD defensive system: "what to move", "how to move" and "when to move".

"What to move" describes which network configuration parameters can be changed to hinder an attacker's offense. Common changeable configuration parameters include: open port, IP address, and transmission route etc. By altering these settings, the attack surface is altered, which raises the assault time cost and slows the attacker's attack progress. It should be mentioned that, in the majority of circumstances, the defender must choose suitable dynamic parameters based on the network scenario and the kind of attack faced. hey must also satisfy the network's communication demands while obstructing the attacker's attempt. In addition, to stop the attacker from inferring the configuration values through brute-force cracking, the adjustable range of the selected parameters should be as large as possible to increase the difficulty of cracking.

"How to move" refers to the way in which configuration parameters are changed to confuse the attacker. The way to move parameters needs to emphasise randomness. The main purpose is to let the attacker can not master the rule of parameter change. At the same time, it is crucial to minimize the influence on the present network system's quality in light of the current threat scenario by using

1.3 Overview of Network-Based Moving Target Defense 7

low-costmobile solutions. Artificial Intelligence (AI) technology has emerged as a low-cost, highly flexible answer to the "how to move" challenge. Ref. [17] have begun to apply AI techniques to MTDs to improve their defence efficiency and adaptability.

"When to move" describes the time that has been decided upon to change the network configuration. Different MTD methods will adopt different time-shifting strategies. Traditional MTD methods choose a fixed time period to move the configuration. There are also some methods that choose variable time period to move the configuration. They choose purely random time period to adjust [18] or adaptively adjust the network configuration parameters according to the malicious behavior [19].

1.3.2 Methods Classification

In this section, we categorize the current network-based MTD methods into three types from the perspective of network operation mechanisms: active virtual migration, proxy shuffle, and network property mutation, followed by a brief introduction to each.

1.3.2.1 Active Virtual Migration

Active virtual migration moves instances of virtual resources, such as virtual machines and containers, on a regular basis, making it harder for attackers to find their target. For example, in order to prevent side channel attacks, Qiang et al. [20] presented a dynamic heterogeneous redundancy model that will force MANO to periodically relocate the VNF components on each VM. The memory capacity of each virtual machine (VM) and the size of the service during the migration period determine how long the migration takes for each VM. Samir et al. [21] provide a method that regularly finds vulnerabilities at every system location and assesses the total risk level everywhere in real time. This mechanism will direct the MTD strategy to support runtime real-time migration of virtual SDN controllers between locations.

1.3.2.2 Proxy Shuffling

Proxy Shuffling disrupts an attacker's path discovery process by frequently changing the distribution or mapping relationships of proxy servers in the network. The primary purpose of this technique is to protect against distributed denial of service (DDoS) attacks. the MTD dynamically adjusts the association relationship between users and proxies. If an agent is not attacked, the users connected to it can be considered as normal users. Then by shuffling the remaining users among the agents, the spy users will be gradually recognized and blocked, thus guaranteeing the network service quality. For example, Zhou et al. [22] mitigated DDoS attacks by forcing attackers to be isolated to as few edge nodes as possible through service migration in an industrial Internet of Things (IIoT) scenario. Yan et al. [23] dynamically adjusted the mapping relationship between users and proxies and switch the communication agents when necessary. To achieve seamless agent switching, the article employs an overlay-based wrapping mechanism and an independent sidecar implementation. Yan et al. [24] considered the reverse proxy as a moving target, and employed a mix-and-match mechanism to change the relationship between users and reversed proxies to achieve low-cost defense against DDoS attacks.

1.3.2.3 Network Property Mutation

Network property mutation is a defense method that confuses or hinders attackers by dynamically changing network properties. This method can be subdivided into host mutation and route mutation.

Host mutation prevents an attacker from precisely identifying and locating the target system by periodically changing key characteristic information about the host. This approach can act at multiple levels of the network:

- At the network layer, the system's IP address might change over time, making it challenging for an attacker to pinpoint a target for further attacks.
- At the transport layer, the system may dynamically adjust the port number of a service, preventing an attacker from utilizing fixed port information for vulnerability exploitation.
- At the application layer, the system may change device fingerprints or user identifiers, rendering attacks based on identity tracking ineffective.

For example, Jafarian et al. [25] analyzed and portrayed malicious scanning behaviors through hypothesis testing, and then dynamically modified host IP addresses to hinder detection of attacks. Bharathi et al. [26] applied Lorenz chaos theory to MTD in SDN environments, which used three mechanisms, including port mutation, IP mutation and route mutation, to achieve a dynamic randomization of network configurations.

Route mutation is used to make it harder for attackers to foresee and intercept traffic by dynamically changing the transmission path of packets in the network. This approach is designed to counter attacks targeting the network layer [27], such as DDoS attacks, man-in-the-middle attacks and traffic monitoring. Specifically, it can be subdivided into base on satisfiability modulo theory (SMT) routing mutation and diverse routing mutation. In terms of SMT-based routing mutation, Zhou et al. [28] used SMT for the first time to model the random routing variability problem as a constraint satisfaction problem to achieve feasible routing mutation. Based on this study, Gillani et al. [29] introduced the crossfire attack model as one of the constraints of SMT, which increases the decision uncertainty of attackers and effectively reduces the threat of DDoS attacks. Diverse routing mutation, on the other hand, focuses more on improving defense effectiveness by increasing routing diversity and dynamics. Aydeger et al. [30], for instance, presented a framework to build virtual shadow networks through NFV to simulate diverse network environments, and dynamically change the routes to organize the attacker to identify the actual DDoS network topology, and simultaneously makes it easier for the defender to forensically confirm the information provided by the attacker.

1.4 Organization of the Book

This book introduces AI techniques to MTD systems and provides a technical exploration of intelligent active defense systems. The book's remaining sections are arranged as follows:

In Chap. 2, we design a host address mutation (HAM) scheme based on AI technique. The MTD method of HAM has been proposed in order to counter network reconnaissance attacks. But it now suffers from the following problems: (1) the inability to adapt itself to counter strategies; (2) the fact that each host can decide at any time whether or not to change its IP address will cause drastic changes in network conditions; (3) the disregard for how long-lasting current communication links are. This chapter presents a deep reinforcement learning (DRL) approach to enhance HAM in order to address the aforementioned issues. First, we build a Markov Decision Process (MDP) to characterize the mutation process. Then, we transform the address-to-host assignment equation into a constraint satisfaction problem to remove the inactionable actions in the action space of the MDP. Meanwhile, we design a advantage actor-critic algorithm to make our proposed MTD method learn from the scanning behavior thus improving the defense performance.

In Chap. 3, we investigate MTD defense schemes in Digital Twin Mobile Network (DTMN). Traditional MTD applied to DTMN suffers from the following problems: (1) insufficient performance of collaborative scheduling among multiple MTD schemes; (2) insufficient consideration of time allocation for multiple MTD schemes; and (3) the current defense strategy only considers current information, not future information. We suggest MTD based on collaborative mutation to address the aforementioned issues. Route Mutation (RM) and HAM are two MTD systems that we consider. We construct a semi-Markov decision process (SMDP) to describe time-varying security events and dynamic deployment of various MTDs. Then, we use Long Short-Term Memory (LSTM) to foresee security events and use these events as the network state of the SDMP. Then, using SMT, the problem of assigning IP address space and choosing alternative routes is described as a constraint satisfaction problem. This problem is then addressed to exclude inactionable actions from the MDP action space. Finally, we also design a hierarchical DRL algorithm for coordinated scheduling.

In Chap. 4, we investigate MTD in a Software defined Internet of vehicles (SD-IoV). Current MTDs applied in SD-IoV suffer from the following problems: (1) lack of intellect; (2) incapacity to manage extremely dynamic circumstances; and (3) difficulties tracing sources. We provide a smart MTD method in this chapter to solve the aforementioned issues. We use DRL to solve for the ideal configuration after first modeling the configuration modification of roadside units (RSUs) as MDPs. After shuffling, we then assess the vehicles' reliability in order to identify the spy cars.

In Chap. 5, we use RM to counter packet drop attacks in Vehicular Ad hoc Networks (VANETs). We design an extended grid-based joint action learning approach to implement RM in VANETs. We introduce Multi-Agent Reinforcement Learning (MARL) into RM and improve the existing MARL for the network characteristics of VANETs, making it online and adaptive. Our proposed scheme accelerates learning convergence through parameter sharing. In this scheme, the target region is uniformly divided into a grid. When a vehicle transmits a data packet, the learning strategy prioritizes the next-hop node with the smallest movement angle to ensure that it is located within the optimal grid.

In Chap. 6, we provide an overview of the entire book and outline potential paths for further study in the area.

References

1. Zhou, D., Sheng, M., Li, J., Han, Z.: Aerospace integrated networks innovation for empowering 6g: a survey and future challenges. IEEE Commun. Surv. Tutor. **25**(2), 975–1019 (2023)
2. Guo, J., Bilal, M., Qiu, Y., Qian, C., Xu, X., Raymond Choo, K.-K.: Survey on digital twins for internet of vehicles: fundamentals, challenges, and opportunities. Digit. Commun. Netw. **10**(2), 237–247 (2024)
3. Priyadarshi, R.: Energy-efficient routing in wireless sensor networks: a meta-heuristic and artificial intelligence-based approach: a comprehensive review. Arch. Comput. Methods Eng. **31**(4), 2109–2137 (2024)
4. Ding, W., Abdel-Basset, M., Ali, A.M., Moustafa, N.: Large language models for cyber resilience: a comprehensive review, challenges, and future perspectives. Appl. Soft Comput. **170**, 112663 (2025)
5. Sun, Z., Sun, G., Liu, Y., Wang, J., Cao, D.: Bargain-match: a game theoretical approach for resource allocation and task offloading in vehicular edge computing networks. IEEE Trans. Mob. Comput. **23**(2), 1655–1673 (2024)
6. Zheng, Y., Li, Z., Xu, X., Zhao, Q.: Dynamic defenses in cyber security: techniques, methods and challenges. Digit. Commun. Netw. **8**(4), 422–435 (2022)
7. Tan, J., Jin, H., Zhang, H., Zhang, Y., Chang, D., Liu, X., Zhang, H.: A survey: when moving target defense meets game theory. Comput. Sci. Rev. **48**, 100544 (2023)
8. Ding, C., Zhou, A., Liu, Y., Chang, R.N., Hsu, C.-H., Wang, S.: A cloud-edge collaboration framework for cognitive service. IEEE Trans. Cloud Comput. **10**(3), 1489–1499 (2022)
9. Zhang, Y., Jiang, C., Zhang, P.: Security-aware resource allocation scheme based on drl in cloud–edge–terminal cooperative vehicular network. IEEE Internet Things J. **11**(1), 95–104 (2024)
10. Li, H., Guo, Y., Huo, S., Hu, H., Sun, P.: Defensive deception framework against reconnaissance attacks in the cloud with deep reinforcement learning. Sci. China Inf. Sci. **65**(7), 170305 (2022)
11. Kamaldeep, Malik, M., Dutta, M.: Feature engineering and machine learning framework for ddos attack detection in the standardized internet of things. IEEE Internet Things J. **10**(10), 8658–8669 (2023)

12. Sargolzaei, A., Yazdani, K., Abbaspour, A., Crane III, C.D., Dixon, W.E.: Detection and mitigation of false data injection attacks in networked control systems. IEEE Trans. Ind. Inform. **16**(6), 4281–4292 (2020)
13. Chattopadhyay, A., Mitra, U.: Security against false data-injection attack in cyber-physical systems. IEEE Trans. Control Netw. Syst. **7**(2), 1015–1027 (2020)
14. Manadhata, P.K., Wing, J.M.: An attack surface metric. IEEE Trans. Softw. Eng. **37**(3), 371–386 (2011)
15. Ghosh, A., Pendarakis, D., Sanders, W.: Moving target defense cochair's report-national cyber leap year summit 2009. Technical report, Federal Networking and Information Technology Research and Development (NITRD) Program (2009)
16. Okhravi, H., Hobson, T., Bigelow, D., Streilein, W.: Finding focus in the blur of moving-target techniques. IEEE Secur. Priv. **12**(2), 16–26 (2014)
17. Zhang, T., Xu, C., Zhang, B., Li, X., Kuang, X., Grieco, L.A.: Towards attack-resistant service function chain migration: a model-based adaptive proximal policy optimization approach. IEEE Trans. Dependable Secure Comput. **20**(6), 4913–4927 (2023)
18. Giraldo, J., Cardenas, A., Sanfelice, R.G.: A switching-based moving target defense against sensor attacks in control systems. Nonlinear Anal. Hybrid Syst. **47**, 101268 (2023)
19. Tan, J., Jin, H., Hu, H., Hu, R., Zhang, H., Zhang, H.: Wf-mtd: evolutionary decision method for moving target defense based on wright-fisher process. IEEE Trans. Dependable Secure Comput. **20**(6), 4719–4732 (2023)
20. Qiang, W., Chunming, W., Xincheng, Y., Qiumei, C.: Intrinsic security and self-adaptive cooperative protection enabling cloud native network slicing. IEEE Trans. Netw. Serv. Manag. **18**(2), 1287–1304 (2021)
21. Samir, M., Azab, M., Samir, E.: Sd-cpc: Sdn controller placement camouflage based on stochastic game for moving-target defense. Comput. Commun. **168**, 75–92 (2021)
22. Zhou, Y., Cheng, G., Zhao, Y., Chen, Z., Jiang, S.: Toward proactive and efficient ddos mitigation in iiot systems: a moving target defense approach. IEEE Trans. Ind. Inform. **18**(4), 2734–2744 (2022)
23. Yan, L., Zhou, Z., Yang, S., Xu, C.: Device-cloud collaborative ddos resistance for qos-sensitive mobile applications: a seamlessly shuffle-based moving target defense approach. In: GLOBECOM 2024–2024 IEEE Global Communications Conference, pp. 1191–1196 (2024)
24. Yan, L., Zhou, Z., Yang, S., Xu, C.: Eclipsefortify: imperceptible shuffle-based moving target defense for budget-friendly web service ddos protection. In: 2024 IEEE International Conference on Web Services (ICWS), pp. 1390–1396 (2024)
25. Jafarian, J.H., Al-Shaer, E., Duan, Q.: An effective address mutation approach for disrupting reconnaissance attacks. IEEE Trans. Inf. Forensics Secur. **10**(12), 2562–2577 (2015)
26. Bharathi, N.A., Parthasarathi, R., Vetriselvi, V.: Defending against multifaceted network attacks: a multi-label meta-learning and lorenz chaos mtd based security paradigm. J. Netw. Syst. Manag. **33**(2), 47 (2025)
27. Zhou, Z., Xu, C., Kuang, X., Zhang, T., Sun, L.: An efficient and agile spatio-temporal route mutation moving target defense mechanism. In: ICC 2019–2019 IEEE International Conference on Communications (ICC), pp. 1–6 (2019)
28. Duan, Q., Al-Shaer, E., Jafarian, H.: Efficient random route mutation considering flow and network constraints. In: 2013 IEEE Conference on Communications and Network Security (CNS), pp. 260–268 (2013)
29. Gillani, F., Al-Shaer, E., Lo, S., Duan, Q., Ammar, M., Zegura, E.: Agile virtualized infrastructure to proactively defend against cyber attacks. In: 2015 IEEE Conference on Computer Communications (INFOCOM), pp. 729–737 (2015)
30. Aydeger, A., Saputro, N., Akkaya, K.: A moving target defense and network forensics framework for isp networks using sdn and nfv. Future Gener. Comput. Syst. **94**, 496–509 (2019)

Chapter 2
AI-Driven Moving Target Defense: Host Address Mutation Based on Advantage Actor-Critic Approach

Abstract Large amounts of sensitive and important data are at danger of cyberattacks, which are typically preceded by network reconnaissance, due to the Internet's fast expansion. HAM, a moving target defense strategy, aids in combating network reconnaissance. Nonetheless, HAM continues to face a number of serious issues: (1) Existing methods are unable to adjust to hostile tactics on their own. (2) Because each host chooses whether to change its IP address, the network state varies over time. (3) The majority of approaches disregard the viability of current connections in favor of improving security. In this paper, The aforementioned issues are addressed by proposing an Intelligence-Driven Host Address Mutation (ID-HAM) scheme. To clarify the mutation process, we first build a MDP and create a smooth mutation mechanism. Second, to remove impractical actions from the MDP action space, we formulate address-to-host assignments as a constrained satisfaction issue. Thirdly, in order to learn from scanning behaviors, we create an advantage actor-critic algorithm for HAM. Finally, thorough simulations and security analysis show how effective ID-HAM is. When compared to state-of-the-art systems, ID-HAM can cut scanning hit times by up to 25% with only a slight impact on communication. In order to test various scanning technologies, we also put in place a proof-of-concept prototype system.

Keywords Moving target defense · Host address mutation · Network reconnaissance · Deep reinforcement learning

2.1 Introduction

2.1.1 Motivations

Network security is directly related to quality of service (QoS) of network services and the availability. However, various types of cyber-attacks, especially Advanced Persistent Threat (APT), have always posed serious challenges to current cybersecurity. According to the Attack Report, network service downtime due to DDoS attacks caused a loss of $22,183,680 in mid-2018. Ensuring the security of end-to-end communications is therefore particularly important today [1].

According to [2], cyber reconnaissance is a necessary step in the cyber kill chain before an attack can be launched that penetrates the target's defenses. Attackers use reconnaissance behaviors to obtain information about the attack target and exploitable vulnerabilities before executing further attacks. Therefore, the security of cyber-physical systems can be greatly improved by disabling the information obtained by attackers through cyber reconnaissance.

2.1.2 Challenges

A new MTD strategy known as HAM [3–7] was put forth as a revolutionary method to disrupt network reconnaissance. HAM seeks to alter hosts' IP addresses on a regular basis in order to make the cyber-physical system more complicated, diverse, and random. Furthermore, HAM is able to supports current communication paradigms rather than changing them, making it appropriate for end-to-end communication.

Unlucky, in order to increase HAM's adaptability and flexibility, three issues must be researched and resolved. The first and most important issue is that altered IP addresses and blind host assignments will waste network resources without making HAM more unpredictable. This is because current approaches cannot adapt to hostile tactics on their own. Second, hosts have the option of switching IP addresses because HAM adds additional network overheads. As a result of the hosts' dynamic decisions, network conditions will usually show wide changes. Thirdly, HAM techniques typically overlook the endurance of system communications in favor of an overemphasis on system security concerns. Lean and efficient HAM approaches are necessary since many network services have high QoS requirements.

2.1.3 Contributions

This paper proposes an **I**ntelligence **D**riven **H**ost **A**ddress **M**utation (**ID-HAM**) to address the aforementioned issues. Unlike any other existing methods, we intelligently slow down network reconnaissance by designing a HAM system based on DRL. Many security problems have been resolved using reinforcement learning (RL) [8, 9], such as the deployment of honeypots, secure offloading, and so on. Furthermore, since SDN is able to offer dynamic programming for flow control and flexible network administration, we take it to improve the viability of ID-HAM [10, 11]. As far as we are aware, our work is the sole attempt to apply DRL to HAM challenges in a way that balances end-to-end quality of service requirements and communication security.

The main contributions of this study may be summed up as follows:

1. In HAM, a MDP-based model is used for describing time-varying network conditions. Our work's primary objective is to model MDP for the mutation process in a concrete manner. We characterize actions as the reorganization of host-to-host assignments, state transitions as the quantity of hosts that alter their IP addresses, and network state as the categories of hosts.
2. In order to maintain live connections, the HAM communication mechanism is created to guarantee smooth address mutation. Constrained satisfaction problems are used to describe address-to-host assignments, accounting for various real-world constraints including mutation rate, flow table size, and forbidden block. Eliminating unsuitable activities from MDP's action space is the goal.
3. Based on the MDP specifications, we first construct an advantage actor-critic algorithm for HAM to shuffle address-to-host allocations. Then, in accordance with varying mutation rates, mutated IP addresses will be selected on a regular basis to correlate with hosts. ID-HAM seeks to learn from scanning behaviors in order to greatly enhance defense performance.
4. To verify the efficacy of ID-HAM, a comprehensive set of Mininet simulations and security analysis are conducted. Additionally, We built a proof-of-concept prototype system to test our proposed method using multiple scanning instruments. Overall, as compared to the most advanced systems, our suggested ID-HAM can reduce scanning hit times by up to 25% while just marginally affecting communication quality of service.

2.1.4 Related Work

Techniques for defensive deception involve taking steps to mislead or confuse the enemy, which makes it execute pointless activities. In order to trick attackers into believing that valuable hosts have been located, Xing et al. [12] designed a method that hiding active hosts and trapping them into decoy nodes. However, static deployment policy severely limits the effectiveness of various deception techniques, making it easy for the adversary to identify and circumvent deception resources.

HAM is thought to be the most excellent instance of an MTD technology that disrupts network reconnaissance. It was suggested by Sharma et al. [4] to change genuine IP addresses into time-varying and random ones. HAM was used in numerous SDN controllers or SDN-based in-vehicle networks in other works [5, 6]. These approaches may waste network resources without lowering system vulnerabilities since they are unable to adapt automatically to scanning procedures [13]. Jafarian et al. [7] suggested altering end-hosts' IP addresses through the use of hypothesis testing to examine and describe hostile actions. Although this approach can somewhat adapt to malevolent actions, its dynamical adjustment capabilities are still constrained.

RL has been used in numerous studies to address security issues in recent years. An intelligent deployment method was developed by Wang et al. [8] to adjust the placement of decoy nodes according to security conditions. To establish a safe edge caching framework, Xu et al. [9] suggested building a Stackelberg game model with edge caching devices and content providers. The best course of action is then determined using the Q-learning algorithm. Our earlier research [1, 14, 15] suggested RL-based intelligent MTD strategies, demonstrating that RL may greatly enhance defense performance. In order to protect against DDoS, the work in [1, 14] concentrated on dynamically modifying the paths of different flows. A client-to-proxy shuffling method that continuously switches proxies was proposed by the work in [15] to stop DDoS attacks on online service systems. It is evident that a number of the aspects in the current work change from those in earlier work, such as the MTD framework, the threat type taken into consideration, and the design of the MTD strategy. Furthermore, the current work uses a proof-of-concept prototype system to do tests, in contrast to simulations in previous work.

In fact, RL has demonstrated its ability to make effective judgments by optimizing the environment's cumulative reward. So we think that RL shows potential in addressing HAM difficulties, such as resolving the MTD problem of *"how to move.* This is so that RL can continuously learn from adversarial attack behaviors to optimize mutation selection and thus better adapt to multiple adversarial attack strategies. As far as we are aware, our study is the primary effort to suggest a DRL-based HAM scheme that meets both security and QoS requirements in end-to-end communication.

2.2 Model Formulation on the Cloud Layer

The threat, network, and MDP models that serve as the foundation for the HAM scheme's architecture are described in depth in this section. To effectively implement our proposed scheme, we leverage the programmable of SDN to achieve dynamic and adaptive address transformation by separating the network control and forwarding functions.

2.2.1 Threat Model

Insider reconnaissance is the subject of this paper. In this scenario, at least one host in the internal network is often under the attacker's initial control. In existing literature, this assumption is widely used [12, 16, 17]. The external adversary can do this by manually infecting the system or by using zero-day vulnerabilities with downloads [16].

Based on the network data gathered during reconnaissance, the adversary will be able to propagate the attack if any insider hosts have been compromised. This is due to the fact that before acquiring insider access, the attacker usually knows nothing about the internal network. Reconnaissance aims to collect critical network information from an internal network, including service dependencies, unpatched

2.2 Model Formulation on the Cloud Layer

vulnerabilities, open ports, and active hosts. Regretfully, some scanning programs such as Nmap [18] are capable of sending probing queries to connectable hosts within the network of network. The attacker causes serious harm by executing simultaneous cyber kill chains on the targets they have targeted using the network data they have collected.

It is also assumed that the number and location of malicious hosts in the network are unknown. The scanning process can be described by two primary factors: (1) the address space that the attacker looks for active hosts in is known as the scanning space; (2) scanning rate, or how many IP addresses can be scanned in a specific period of time. Rapid scanning is frequently low-rate, stealthy, and persistent because it is easy to detect.

In actuality, there is an extremely disparate distribution of susceptible hosts throughout the network. As a result, scanning strategies determine how to efficiently detect hosts. For a crafty adversary, we look at the following scanning methods:

1. **Local preference scanning**: random probing requests are sent by the attacker to uniformly probe the network. If the scan is successful, the attacker will then be more inclined to look for IP addresses near active hosts.
2. **Sequential scanning**: the attacker bombards the target network with successive probing queries, but at some point, it will randomly choose its starting IP address again.
3. **Divide-conquer scanning**: the attacker simultaneously asks probing inquiries using a group of slave hosts. A sequential scanning strategy is adopted by all slave hosts, and the probability of scanned hosts being compromised as slave hosts is ρ.

2.2.2 Network Model

HAM periodically changes a host's IP address. In SDN, the appropriate Openflow switch (OF-switch) can convert the hosts' real IP (rIP) addresses into virtual IP (vIP) addresses.

Assume that SDN is divided into z subnets, represented by the notation $\{S_1, \cdots, S_z\}$. A collection of hosts that share an OF-switch are referred to as a subnet. A set of n hosts $\{h_1, \cdots, h_n\}$ make up the entire network. Two types of hosts are known to exist: (1) Moving hosts, whose vIP addresses change on a regular basis; (2) Static hosts: these hosts' vIP addresses remain constant. The modified address space Ω is obtained by removing utilized vIP addresses, such as broadcasting addresses, from the full address space A:

$$\Omega \leftarrow A \wedge \neg(A_1 \vee \cdots \vee A_u), \tag{2.1}$$

where used vIP addresses are indicated by $A_1, \cdots, A_u$. Moreover, unused address ranges can be utilized to form m IP address blocks of size $\mathcal{Z}$. In the address space, IP address blocks are represented by the notation $r_1, r_2, \cdots, r_m$, where each IP address is distinct. We establish two tiers to increase HAM's unpredictability:

Address Block Shuffling (AS) Shuffled IP address blocks are sent to hosts according to a variety of criteria, including network security and functioning, as described at the top level. The system parameter T^{AS} indicates the AS assignment interval, which determines how IP address blocks are allocated to hosts.

Random vIP Mutation The lower level focuses on changing vIP addresses linked to mobile hosts. For a specific host h_i, the re-mapping interval T_i^{RM} serves as its parameter. To prevent IP address conflicts, the modified vIP addresses are selected from the matching IP address blocks. Furthermore, the system parameter T^{AS} is composed of multiple T_i^{RM} values.

2.2.3 Markov Decision Process Model

Temporal dynamics are described by dividing time into equal slots. The fundamental definition of a time slot is $\Delta T = \min_{i \in n} T_i^{RM}$. Then, $T_i = \lceil T_i^{RM}/\Delta T \rceil$ is used to determine the amount of time slots in T_i^{RM}. The index $t \in \{0, 1, 2, \cdots\}$ will slot time according to the definition of ΔT. To account for dynamic transitions between stationary and mobile hosts, we construct the mutation process as MDP in this subsection. In contrast to earlier work [19] that models MDP for MTD from a high and abstraction level, our study focuses on modeling MDP from a real level. The following are MDP's salient features:

2.2.3.1 Network State Space

The network's overall state is influenced by the many host types operating inside it. The network state is represented as a vector $S_t = \{s_1, \cdots, s_n\}$, where $s_i = 1$ ($1 \leq i \leq n$) indicates that the i-th host is a moving host, and $s_i = 0$ indicates that the i-th host is a static host. Since each host has two statuses, the overall amount of network states will be $\Gamma = 2^n$. This means that $\{S_1, \cdots, S_\Gamma\}$ is a description of the network state space. Each host sends a signal packet to the specified IP address after deciding to run or shut down the HAM scheme on its own. This will not be linked to any host. It is just considered the destination of signal packets. Upon receipt of this packet, the OF-switch will communicate with the SDN controller to ascertain the packet's forwarding destination. The SDN controller detects the packet's distinct IP address and acquires signal data on any changes to the host's IP address. Lastly, the SDN controller will drop the signal packet.

2.2 Model Formulation on the Cloud Layer

2.2.3.2 Action Space

The allotment of IP address blocks is the first choice made at each T^{AS}. The assignment of IP address blocks to all hosts is described as an action $\mathcal{A}_t = \{a_{1,1}, \cdots, a_{i,k}, \cdots, a_{n,m}\}$, where $a_{i,k} = 1$ ($1 \leq i \leq n, 1 \leq k \leq m$) indicates that the k-th IP address block is allocated to the i-th host, and $a_{i,k} = 0$ indicates otherwise. Keep in mind that activities have a space complexity of 2^{nm}, which will rise exponentially with the number of IP address blocks or hosts. However, many activities can be referred to as *infeasible actions* since they do not satisfy network restrictions. See Sect. 2.3.1 for more information on constraint formalization. $\{\mathcal{A}_1, \cdots, \mathcal{A}_L\}$ is the action space, assuming that there are L possible allocations in total. Second, while static hosts maintain vIPs unchanged, moving hosts randomly alter vIPs selected from allotted IP address blocks.

2.2.3.3 State Transitions

The concept of network state states that, under the assumption that the number of hosts stays constant, a state transition happens when the number of moving hosts rises or falls. We assume, for simplicity, that a static host has a likelihood of $\mathcal{P}_s$ transferring into a moving host at each T^{AS}, and a moving host has the likelihood of $\mathcal{P}_m$ transferring to a static host. Whether or not the adversary effectively scans the host determines the values of $\mathcal{P}_s$ and $\mathcal{P}_m$.

2.2.3.4 Reward Function

Reward should be monitored once the action is chosen in order to inform subsequent decisions. According to intrusion detection techniques [20–22], scanning operations will be precisely detected after they take place. Consequently, in order to increase the likelihood of avoiding scans, we describe the reward function that is impacted by scanning behaviours as follows:

$$\mathcal{R}_t = \begin{cases} -\alpha \sum_{i \in n} \Theta_i, & \text{if hosts are scanned successfully,} \\ C, & \text{if hosts avoid scanning,} \end{cases} \quad (2.2)$$

where α represents a coefficient, Θ_i denotes the number of successful scans on host h_i during a T^{AS} interval, and C is a positive constant. Based on this reward function, the reward for properly scanned hosts will be a negative number that is linearly connected to Θ_i. Otherwise, if hosts don't scan, we will get a positive continuous reward.

2.3 Detailed Design

The mutation strategy generated by DRL, which learns scanning behaviours for optimal mutation selection, is implemented by our suggested ID-HAM, as illustrated in Fig. 2.1. To gather network data, the SDN controller keeps an eye on the substrate network. The two primary components of ID-HAM are as follows in order to make efficient mutation decisions:

1. **Address Block Allocation Formalization**: We want to eliminate activities that are not feasible from the action space of MDP by formalising the allocation of address blocks based on SMT [23]. Next, we resolve the constrained satisfaction issue using the Z3 theorem prover [24]. These solutions are workable address-to-host configurations that meet a number of requirements. Additional information is explained in Sect. 2.3.1.
2. **Intelligent HAM Algorithm**: We create a framework for HAM that combines advantage actor-critic algorithm. In order to increase the unpredictability, this algorithm will learn from the scanning approach to allocate IP address blocks to hosts. A thorough illustration of ID-HAM can be seen in Sect. 2.3.2.

2.3.1 Address Allocation Formalization

The assignment of IP address blocks $\{r_1, r_2, \cdots, r_m\}$ to all hosts is formalized as a restricted satisfaction issue based on SMT in this subsection. assuming that the binary variable b_i^k indicates whether host h_i is assigned IP address block r_k. If this is the case, b_i^k equals 1; if not, b_i^k equals 0. Viable IP address block allocations should meet many requirements based on real-world network conditions [7], which are expressed as follows:

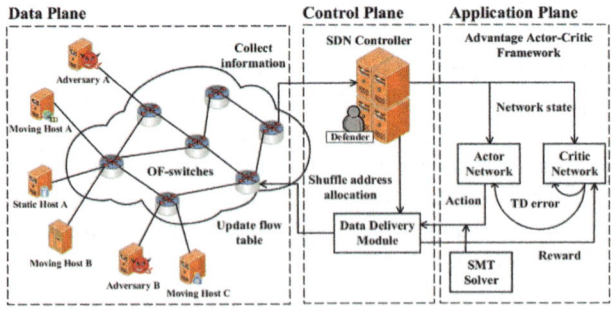

Fig. 2.1 System framework of ID-HAM in SDN

2.3 Detailed Design

2.3.1.1 Mutation Rate Constraint

When there is a set amount of IP address blocks, a high mutation rate indicates that a vIP has an elevated likelihood of being chosen more than once. As a result, host h_i must have an IP address block count so that the average repeating probability equals 0. The following represents the amount of mutations for shifting host h_i during a T^{AS}:

$$\mathcal{N}_i = \lceil T^{AS}/T_i^{RM} \rceil. \tag{2.3}$$

The likelihood of recurring is represented as follows when choosing the $\mathcal{Y}$-th vIP address after uniformly choosing the $\mathcal{Y} - 1$ vIP addresses:

$$\mathcal{P}_{i,\mathcal{Y}} = \frac{\mathcal{Y} - 1}{(\sum_{k=1}^{m} b_i^k)\mathcal{Z}}, \tag{2.4}$$

where the size of the IP address block is $\mathcal{Z}$. Next, the predicted value of the repeat probability is then calculated using the formula below:

$$\mathbb{E}[\mathcal{P}_{i,\mathcal{Y}}] = \frac{1}{\mathcal{N}_i} \sum_{\mathcal{Y}=1}^{\mathcal{N}_i} \mathcal{P}_{i,\mathcal{Y}} = \frac{\mathcal{N}_i - 1}{2\mathcal{Z}(\sum_{k=1}^{m} b_i^k)}. \tag{2.5}$$

The mutation rate limitation is expressed as follows, assuming that ω is the upper limit of the repeating probability:

$$\sum_{k=1}^{m} b_i^k \geq \lceil \frac{\mathcal{N}_i - 1}{2\mathcal{Z}\omega} \rceil, \tag{2.6}$$

where the lowest amount of IP address blocks that needs to be assigned to host h_i in order to achieve the intended repeating probability is $\lceil (\mathcal{N}_i - 1)/2\mathcal{Z}\omega \rceil$.

2.3.1.2 Forbidden Block Constraint

Blocks that are prohibited from being utilized for mutation due to operational limitations must be avoided when allocating address blocks. The collection of forbidden blocks is defined as $\mathcal{F}$. The following is the expression for the forbade block restriction:

$$\sum_{i=1}^{n} b_i^k = 1, \forall r_k \in (\Omega - \mathcal{F}), \tag{2.7}$$

$$b_i^k = 0, \ if \ r_k \in \mathcal{F}. \tag{2.8}$$

According to Eq. (2.7), an IP address block that is not in the banned set can only be issued to a single host. IP address blocks in the banned set cannot be allocated to any host, according to Eq. (2.8).

2.3.1.3 Flow Table Size Constraint

The flow tables of OF-switches require being updated once IP address blocks shift to other hosts. To decrease the flow table's size, supernetting will combine nearby blocks that are allocated to the same OF-switch into bigger ones. Supernetting is required to achieve the QoS requirement because it can lower network management overheads.

To indicate if IP address block r_k has been assigned to a minimum of one host in subnet S_i, we use the binary variable $\mathcal{W}_i^k$:

$$\mathcal{W}_i^k = \bigvee_{h_i \in S_i} b_i^k. \tag{2.9}$$

$\mathcal{D}_{k_1,k_2}$ is a variable that indicates whether IP address blocks r_{k_1} and r_{k_2} are next to one other. Then, to indicate whether IP address blocks r_{k_1} and r_{k_2} are contiguous and both allocated to subnet S_i, we define $\mathcal{L}_i^{k_1,k_2}$ as a binary variable:

$$\mathcal{L}_i^{k_1,k_2} = \mathcal{W}_i^{k_1} \wedge \mathcal{W}_i^{k_2} \wedge \mathcal{D}_{k_1,k_2}. \tag{2.10}$$

OF-switches will do timely lookups when the flow table is not very huge. The restriction of this flow table size is expressed as follows:

$$\sum_{k_1} \sum_{k_2 \neq k_1} \mathcal{L}_i^{k_1,k_2} \geq \Psi, \tag{2.11}$$

where the total amount of neighbouring address blocks given to the identical OF-switch is at least Ψ.

2.3.1.4 Solution Principle of Address Block Allocation

Finding solutions that meet the aforementioned limitations is usually an NP-complete satisfiability issue [7] because assignment decision b_i^k only takes a value from {0, 1}. The computational and communication resources of SDN controllers are restricted [1]. In the meantime, it will take an extensive amount of time and resources to solve this satisfiability issue in real time.

Since topology changes are typically costly and time-consuming, wired network topologies typically do not undergo drastic changes [25]. Therefore, we will use the Z3 solver [24], the most recent theorem prover created by Microsoft Research,

2.3 Detailed Design

to pre-calculate this difficult possible IP address block allocations issue. The Z3 solver can compute millions of variables and tens of thousands of constraints [23]. Block allocations for possible IP addresses should be updated whenever the network topology changes. These workable assignments are saved in the SDN controller, processed inside the OF-switch configurations beforehand, and triggered when needed. By reducing the total number of viable actions from 2^{nm} to L, the SMT formalisation will improve the convergence speed of DRL and prevent the repeated training of infeasible actions.

2.3.2 Intelligent Host Address Mutation

Due to the fact that advantage actor-critic functions [26] effectively in action space and vast state. we apply it in this study to address the MDP problem given in Sect. 2.2.3. The two primary components of advantage actor-critic are the actor network and the critic network. While the critic network assesses and critiques the present policy using the reward received from the environment, the actor network specifies the parameterised policy and chooses actions depending on the observed state. We provide an estimate of the value function $V(S_t; \theta_c)$ with weight θ_c and the actor policy $\pi(\mathcal{A}_t | S_t; \theta_a)$ as action selection probability with weight θ_a. The actor network's loss function is thus provided by:

$$\mathcal{J}_\pi(\theta_a) = \hat{A}(\mathcal{A}_t, S_t) \log \pi(\mathcal{A}_t | S_t; \theta_a) + \beta \mathcal{H}(\pi(\mathcal{A}_t | S_t; \theta_a)), \quad (2.12)$$

where $\mathcal{H}(\pi(\mathcal{A}_t | S_t; \theta_a))$ is the entropy of action distribution defined as follows:

$$\mathcal{H}(\pi(\mathcal{A}_t | S_t; \theta_a)) = -\sum_{\mathcal{A}} \pi(\mathcal{A}_t | S_t; \theta_a) \log \pi(\mathcal{A}_t | S_t; \theta_a), \quad (2.13)$$

As exploration solely relies on policy sampling, entropy regularisation can be utilised to improve exploring ability. β is the hyperparameter that regulates the degree of strength of the entropy regularisation term, while $\hat{A}(\mathcal{A}_t, S_t)$ is the benefit function, which is defined as follows:

$$\begin{aligned} \hat{A}(\mathcal{A}_t, S_t) &= Q(S_t, \mathcal{A}_t) - V(S_t) \\ &= \mathcal{R}_t + \gamma V(S_{t+1}; \theta_c) - V(S_t; \theta_c), \end{aligned} \quad (2.14)$$

It illustrates the benefit of carrying out action $\mathcal{A}_t$ at state S_t. The following is the result of differentiating the actor network's loss function in (2.14) with regard to weight θ_a:

$$\nabla_{\theta_a} \mathcal{J}_\pi(\theta_a) = \hat{A} \nabla_{\theta_a} \log \pi(\mathcal{A}_t | S_t; \theta_a) + \beta \nabla_{\theta_a} \mathcal{H}(\pi(S_t; \theta_a)). \quad (2.15)$$

Algorithm 1 Advantage actor-critic algorithm for host address mutation
---
1: Initialize weights θ_a and θ_c of actor and critic network.
2: Initialize learning rates α_a and α_c.
3: Initialize discount factor γ, and hyperparameter β.
4: **for** each training epoch $u = 1, 2, \cdots, U$ **do**
5:    Obtain current network state $\mathcal{S}_t$.
6:    **for** each episode $t = 1, 2, \cdots, T$ **do**
7:       Obtain action $\mathcal{A}_t$ according to policy $\pi(\mathcal{A}_t|\mathcal{S}_t;\theta_a)$.
8:       Execute $\mathcal{A}_t$ to shuffle the address block allocation.
9:       **for** each moving host $h_i = 1, 2, \cdots, N_i$ **do**
10:          Moving host mutates vIP address.
11:          Modify the mapping between rIP and vIP.
12:       **end for**
13:       Static hosts keep vIPs without mutation.
14:       Observe reward $\mathcal{R}_t$.
15:       Observe next state $\mathcal{S}_{t+1}$.
16:       Calculate $\hat{A}(\mathcal{A}_t, \mathcal{S}_t) = \mathcal{R}_t + \gamma V(\mathcal{S}_{t+1}) - V(\mathcal{S}_t)$.
17:       Compute policy gradient $\nabla_{\theta_a}\mathcal{J}_\pi(\theta_a)$ with (2.15).
18:       Update gradient $\theta_a = \theta_a + \alpha_a \nabla_{\theta_a}\mathcal{J}_\pi(\theta_a)$.
19:       Compute value gradient $\nabla_{\theta_c}\mathcal{J}_v(\theta_c)$ with (2.17).
20:       Update gradient $\theta_c = \theta_c + \alpha_c \nabla_{\theta_c}\mathcal{J}_v(\theta_c)$.
21:       Update state $\mathcal{S}_t = \mathcal{S}_{t+1}$.
22:    **end for**
23: **end for**

The definition of the critic network's loss function is:

$$\mathcal{J}_v(\theta_c) = (\mathcal{R}_t - V(\mathcal{S}_t; \theta_c))^2. \tag{2.16}$$

Likewise, if we differentiate the critic network's loss function in equation (2.18) according to weight θ_c, we will obtain:

$$\nabla_{\theta_c}\mathcal{J}_v(\theta_c) = 2(\mathcal{R}_t - V(\mathcal{S}_t; \theta_c))\nabla_{\theta_c}V(\mathcal{S}_t; \theta_c). \tag{2.17}$$

Lastly, the RMSProp algorithm [27], which has been extensively utilized in deep learning, can minimize the loss function. The advantage actor-critic based HAM's pseudocode is shown by the **Algorithm 4**. With weights θ_a and θ_c, respectively, the SDN controller first constructs the actor and critic networks (line 1). We initialize the discount factor γ and the learning rates α_a and α_c (line 2–3). The SDN controller receives the signal packets and uses them to determine the current network state $\mathcal{S}_t$ for each training period (lines 4–5). The investigation begins with the network's present status and continues till T time slots have passed, which are referred to as episodes, the exploration begins (line 6). This SDN controller will execute $\mathcal{A}_t$ to shuffle address block assignments after obtaining an action $\mathcal{A}_t$ in accordance with policy $\pi(\mathcal{A}_t|\mathcal{S}_t;\theta_a)$ (lines 7–8). Migrating hosts change vIPs picked from allotted IP address blocks throughout every change period. Static hosts, however, maintain vIPs without mutation (line 13). The mappings between rIPs and matching vIPs are

2.3 Detailed Design

then changed by the SDN controller (lines 9–12). The reward $\mathcal{R}_t$ and the subsequent state $\mathcal{S}_{t+1}$ are then seen by the SDN controller (lines 14–15). These observations will be used to compute the advantage function and update the actor network's as well as critic network's gradients, separately (lines 16–20). Lastly, changes the network state to the following state (line 21).

We then conduct a theoretical examination of ID-HAM's efficacy in thwarting network reconnaissance. Although our goals are different, our security analysis uses a similar proving procedure to [3]. Our study seeks to solve the anticipated time of probes, while the analysis performed in [3] seeks to address the anticipated amount of probes. Furthermore, in contrast to [3], we define the entire modified address space as Ω, the amount of adversaries as Υ, and the scanning number (also known as the scanning speed) at each mutation phase as η. $\Psi = \eta \Upsilon$ represents the overall amount of scanned IP addresses at every mutation phase.

First, we assume that the enemy is unaware of ID-HAM's deployment. As a result, the attacker won't repeatedly scan vIPs. The likelihood of identifying hosts after t time slots when ID-HAM is not implemented is expressed as follows:

$$\mathcal{P}_t = \frac{\Omega - \Psi}{\Omega} \cdot \frac{\Omega - 2\Psi}{\Omega - \Psi} \cdot \ldots \cdot \frac{\Psi}{\Omega - (t-1)\Psi} = \frac{\Psi}{\Omega}, \quad (2.18)$$

where $t \leq \Omega/\Psi$. The following formula determines the probes' anticipated time:

$$\mathbb{E}[t] = \sum_{t=1}^{\Omega/\Psi} t \cdot \frac{\Psi}{\Omega} = \frac{\Omega + \Psi}{2\Psi}. \quad (2.19)$$

Assuming $\Omega \gg \Psi$, $\mathbb{E}[t] \approx 0.5 \frac{\Omega}{\Psi}$. The likelihood of attacker failure at every change period, if the ID-HAM scheme is implemented, is $(\Omega - \Psi)/\Omega$. The following represents the likelihood of finding hosts after t time slots:

$$\mathcal{P}_t = (\frac{\Omega - \Psi}{\Omega})^{t-1} \cdot \frac{\Psi}{\Omega}. \quad (2.20)$$

The anticipated probing time is then computed as follows:

$$\mathbb{E}[t] = \sum_{t=1}^{\Omega/\Psi} t \cdot (\frac{\Omega - \Psi}{\Omega})^{t-1} \cdot \frac{\Psi}{\Omega} + t \cdot (\frac{\Omega - \Psi}{\Omega})^t. \quad (2.21)$$

The following is how Eq. (2.21) would approach when $\Omega \gg \Psi$:

$$(1 - \frac{2}{e}) \cdot \frac{\Omega}{\Psi} + \frac{1}{e} \frac{\Omega}{\Psi} = (1 - \frac{1}{e}) \cdot \frac{\Omega}{\Psi} \approx 0.63 \frac{\Omega}{\Psi}. \quad (2.22)$$

The ID-HAM technique can extend the scanning duration by 26% more than that of a static IP address by comparing Eqs. (2.22) and (2.19). We will also talk about a few conclusions. Together, the number of adversaries Υ, scan rate η, and mutated address space Ω affect the value of $\mathbb{E}[t]$. The anticipated duration of probes will increase with the size of the modified addressable space Ω. In contrast, the predicted duration of the probes will become shorter as the values of η and Υ increase.

Second, we assume that the enemy is aware of ID-HAM's deployment. As a result, vIPs will undergo many scans. The geometrical random parameter with $\mathcal{P} = \Psi/\Omega$ will be used to determine the likelihood of identifying hosts. Then, $1/\mathcal{P} = \Omega/\Psi$ is the estimated duration of probes. The enemy should invest more 58.7% scanning time in comparison to Eq. (2.22).

2.4 Performance Evaluation and Analysis

To demonstrate the efficacy of our suggested ID-HAM, that we run several kinds of simulations then put a prototype system into use. We examine ID-HAM in terms of network performance, defensive performance, convergence performance, and overheads in SMT formalization.

First, we used **Ryu 4.34** [28] for the SDN Controller to deploy ID-HAM onto a Mininet network running version 2.3. We set up a network of 30/100 hosts and 5/30 OF-switches. we generated the network architecture according on the Waxman model with values $\alpha = 0.2$ and $\beta = 0.15$ using Networkx 2.5 [29]. **Tensorflow 1.14** [30] is employed to train both the actor and critic networks in DRL. And then a multimedia server that we set up is capable of offering video-on-demand services. Table 2.1 shows the simulation parameters. We also constructed a proof-of-concept ID-HAM prototype system, as shown in Fig. 2.2. It consists of an SDN controller with an Intel(R) Core(TM) i9-10920X CPU @ 3.5 GHz, an Nvidia GeForce RTX 5000 GPU, and 4 OF-switches called H3C S5560X-30C-EI. Servers and Raspberry Pis are regarded as end-hosts. The Ryu controller, which can be utilized in prototype systems as well as Mininets, implements the ID-HAM scheme.

2.4.1 Defense Performance

One of the most crucial metrics for assessing defensive effectiveness is the average times of scanning hits (TSHs), which are scanned by **Nmap 7.6** [18]. Employing two network settings, we conduct around 3000 episodes of trials. 30 hosts, 50 IP address blocks, and 5 OF-switches make up one network situation. Another one has 100 hosts, 150 IP address blocks, and 30 OF-switches. Using various scanning methodologies, we compute the average TSHs for each episode when FRVM [4, 31], RHM [7, 32], and ID-HAM are implemented, respectively. The most advanced HAM systems are RHM and FRVM. While FRVM transforms rIPs into random and time-varying vIPs, RHM uses hypothesis testing to change IP addresses in order to examine and describe adversarial behaviors.

2.4 Performance Evaluation and Analysis

Table 2.1 Simulation parameters

Parameter	Value or range
Parameters of Waxman model	$\alpha = 0.2, \beta = 0.15$
Number of OF-switches	[5, 30]
Number of hosts	[10, 15, 20, 25, 30, 100]
Number of IP address blocks	[30, 40, 50, 150]
Bandwidth of links	50 Mbps
Size of IP address block	$Z = 128$
Maximum threshold in formula (2.6)	$\phi = 0.25$
Minimum threshold in formula (2.11)	$\psi = 1$
Number of mutations	$N = 64$
Scanning rate	$16 \, hosts/\Delta T$
Actor hidden layers	[256, 256]
Actor activation function	$ReLU$
Critic hidden layers	[256, 256]
Critic activation function	$ReLU$

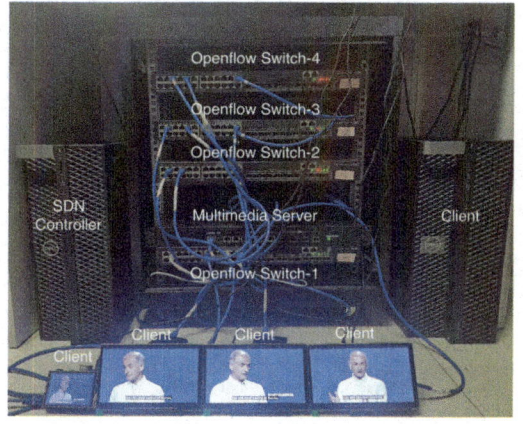

Fig. 2.2 The proof-of-concept prototype system of ID-HAM

Figures 2.3 and 2.4 compare defense performance in a network environment with 50 IP address blocks, 30 hosts, and 5 OF-switches. The average TSH in FRVM, which reaches around 18.6, hardly changes over episodes, as seen in Fig. 2.3a. Until they coincide, the mean TSHs in ID-HAM and RHM similarly decline significantly with episodes. Comparable findings in Fig. 2.3b demonstrate the mean TSHs in RHM drop quickly from 12 to 10.8 as well as mean TSHs in ID-HAM drop gradually from 12 to 9. The mean TSHs in FRVM in this instance are around 12. As seen in Fig. 2.3c, mean TSHs in FRVM exhibit oscillations and rise by around 5.5 times in comparison to those in Fig. 2.3b because divide-conquer scanning is more prone to epidemics than sequential scanning. As ID-HAM learns from scanning activities, average TSHs likewise drop from 17.5 to 14. Finally, Fig. 2.3d shows that mean TSHs in FRVM and RHM are around 19.3 and 19.7, in turn, but mean TSHs in ID-HAM drop from 19.7 to 18. Otherwise, among of the four scanning techniques,

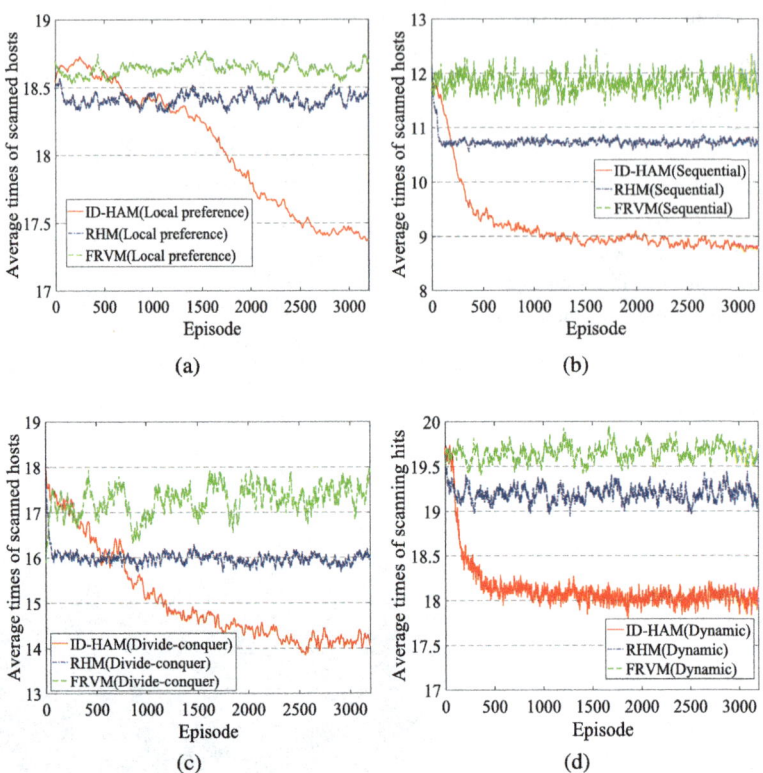

Fig. 2.3 Defense performance comparison when ID-HAM, RHM and FRVM are deployed respectively under network scenario with 5 OF-switches, 30 hosts and 50 IP address blocks. (**a**) Defense performance under local preference scanning. (**b**) Defense performance under sequential scanning. (**c**) Defense performance under divide-conquer scanning. (**d**) Defense performance under dynamic scanning

the mean TSHs in ID-HAM are the highest when the attackers uses the dynamic scanning approach. This is because the dynamic scanning technique has the best scanning performance since it is hard to identify.

The experimental findings comparing the defensive performance of RHM, ID-HAM and FRVM are displayed in Fig. 2.4. Because it is difficult to prevent, this statistic indicates that the changing scanning technique has the highest mean TSHs. As a defense for divide-conquer, localized preference, ordered, and dynamic tactics, ID-HAM lowers mean TSHs by about 1, 3, 4, and 1.7, each, as in comparison with FRVM. The findings show ID-HAM can lower mean TSHs by up to 25%. According to these findings, RHM can adapt to scanning tactics to a certain degree, but ID-HAM's adaptivity is clearly superior to that of FRVM and RHM. Consequently, ID-HAM performs more efficiently in defence.

We then evaluate our prototype system's defensive performance. The intuitive web GUI that allows users to use OF-switches and Ryu controller, adjust the

2.4 Performance Evaluation and Analysis

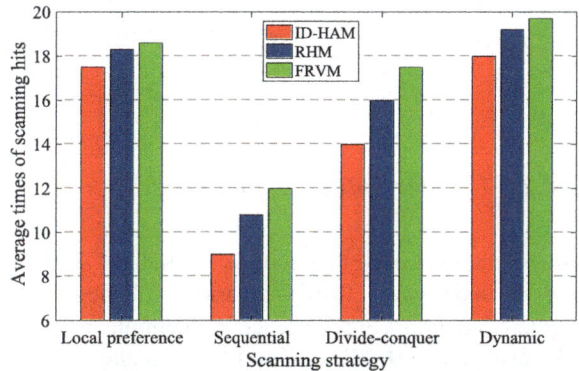

Fig. 2.4 Defense performance comparison of four scanning strategies under network scenario with 5 OF-switches, 30 hosts and 50 IP address blocks

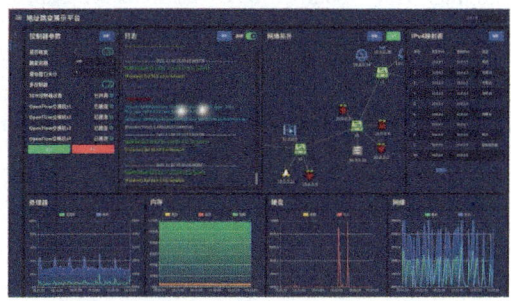

Fig. 2.5 The web-based GUI of ID-HAM

Table 2.2 Comparison among multiple scanning tools

Scanning tool	Nmap	arp-scan	Fping	Netdiscover
Scanning time	4 min	4 min	4 min	4 min
Protocol	ARP	ARP	ICMP	ARP
Number of vIPs	312	312	312	312
Coverage	27.9%	46.8%	29.9%	22.1%

mutation period as well as sliding window, and execute ID-HAM is shown in Fig. 2.5. Additionally, the network topology and real-time logs are displayed appropriately. The network scenario in the prototype system includes 13 hosts and 4 OF-switches. Furthermore, real-time monitoring is done on the mapping connection between rIPs and vIPs as well as resource overheads. **Nmap 7.6** [18], **arp-scan 1.9.7** [33], **Fping 4.2** [34], and **Netdiscover 0.3-beta7** [35] are among the various network scanning tools that we use. These tools search the whole address space on a single host. These results are displayed in Table 2.2.

We selected the mutation time at 10 s and the overall scanning duration at 4 min. Thus, 312 is the total quantity of historical vIPs. We use Nmap's scanning method with "T3" and configure it arp-scan transmitting speed at 4000 bps. In the meantime, we set the Fping and Netdiscover sending intervals to 120 ms and 75 ms, respectively. TSHs for Nmap are 87 with a coverage of around 27.9%. TSHs cost 146 for arp-scan, with coverage of around 46.8%. TSHs for Fping are 93 with a coverage of around 29.9%. TSHs for Netdiscover are 69, with coverage of around

22.1%. Although Netdiscover possesses the lowest scanning convergence, Arp-scan has the biggest. We may infer that ID-HAM could substantially decrease the area of coverage of popular scanning technologies.

2.4.2 Convergence Performance

We use the DRL incentive to assess ID-HAM's converging performance. We assess rewards under two network scenarios while defending against many tactics, such as divide-conquer, local preference, sequential, and dynamic scanning. 5 OF-switches, 30 hosts, and 50 IP address blocks make up one network situation. Another one has 100 hosts, 150 IP address blocks, and 30 OF-switches. According to assessment results, the fastest convergence speed occurs while defending against sequential scanning, as seen in Figs. 2.6 and 2.7. ID-HAM will converge in around 500 episodes. Conversely, while protecting against local preference scanning, the converging speed is the least fast. Under these circumstances, ID-HAM will

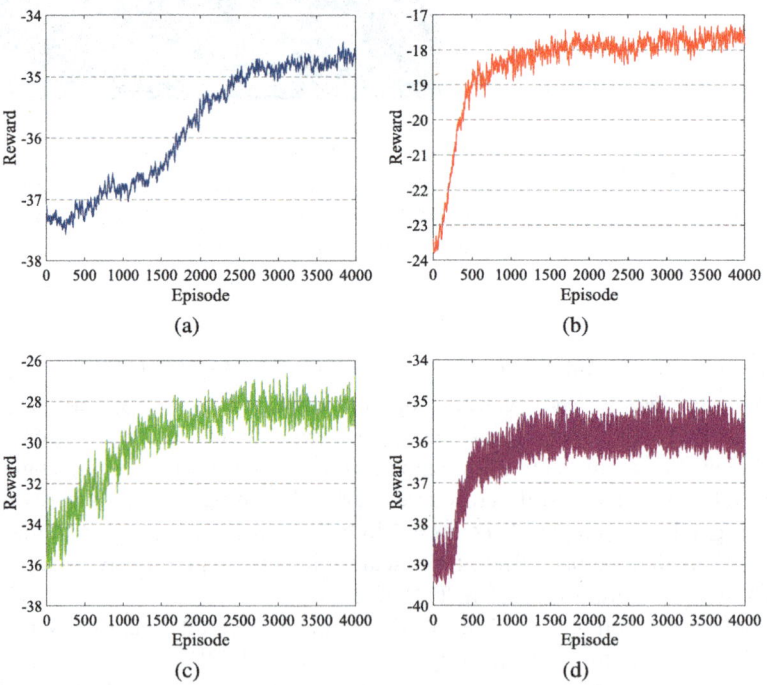

Fig. 2.6 Convergence performance of ID-HAM defending against multiple scanning strategies under network scenario with 5 OF-switches, 30 hosts and 50 IP address blocks. (**a**) Local preference scanning. (**b**) Sequential scanning. (**c**) Divide-conquer scanning. (**d**) Dynamic scanning

2.4 Performance Evaluation and Analysis

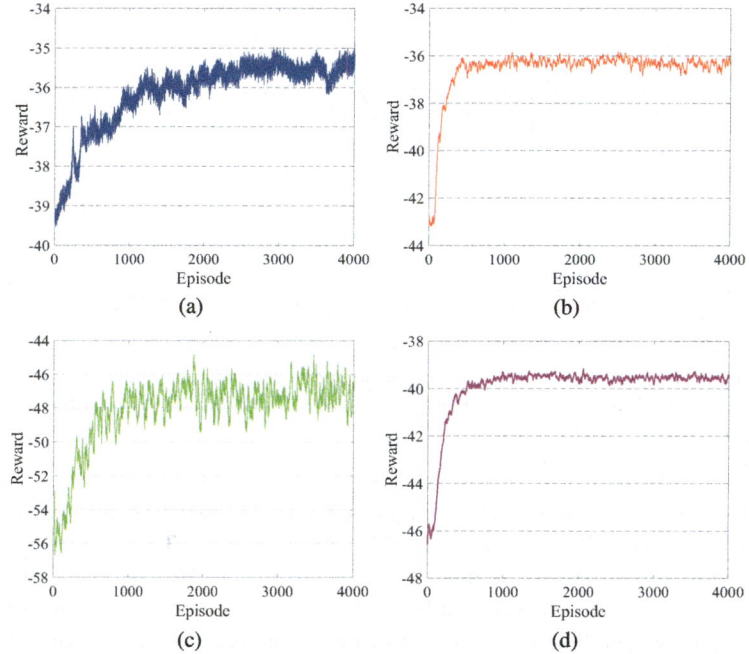

Fig. 2.7 Convergence performance of ID-HAM defending against multiple scanning strategies under network scenario with 30 OF-switches, 100 hosts and 150 IP address blocks. (**a**) Local preference scanning. (**b**) Sequential scanning. (**c**) Divide-conquer scanning. (**d**) Dynamic scanning

converge in around 2500 episodes. In around 2000 episodes, ID-HAM will converge while protecting against divide-conquer scanning. This is due to the fact that localized scanning chooses IP addresses at random to send probe requests in a defined ip space, which is difficult to figure out. The attacker selects IP addresses in a sequential manner during sequential scanning, making it simple to learn from scanning patterns. Furthermore, in two network configurations, DRL's convergence speeds are nearly identical.

2.4.3 Network Performance

We use two measures, mean round-trip time (RTT) and data transfer rate (DTR), both have been evaluated by **iPerf 2.0.10** [36], to assess the network performance of ID-HAM. We configured the mutation time in the video-on-demand service to 5, 10, and 15 s in comparison to no mutation.

The average RTT rises roughly linearly with the number of OF-switches, as Fig. 2.8a shows. The rationale is that a bigger network topology, which is indicated

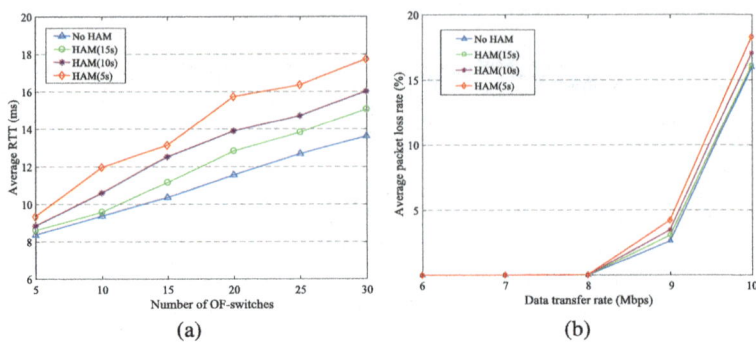

Fig. 2.8 Network performance when mutation period is none, 5 s, 10 s and 15 s. (**a**) Average round-trip time (RTT) for different numbers of OF-switches. (**b**) Average packet loss rate (PLR) for different DTR

by a rising number of OF-switches, would result in a longer transmission path and thus a higher average RTT. In the meanwhile, the average RTT is marginally greater under high mutation rates than under low mutation rates. This is because the SDN controller must update the flow tables in OF-switches due to periodic mutation. A high mutation rate results in more flow table changes, which increases latency. Overall, the average RTT is not significantly impacted by ID-HAM.

According to the results of evaluation in Fig. 2.8b, the mean PLR is about 0 prior to the arrival of 8 Mbps DTR. The average PLR then rises with DTR in an exponential pace. Without ID-HAM installed, the average PLR will be about 16% when DTR comes at 10 Mbps. This is due to the fact that both the forwarding buffer of OF-switches and the bandwidth of connections will restrict DTR and induce packet loss. The findings also show that, in comparison to no mutation, ID-HAM will result in a larger PLR, albeit this increase will be negligible. With ID-HAM implemented and DTR arriving at 10 Mbps, the average PLR will be around 18%, which is a little 2% increase. Consequently, average PLR is not significantly impacted by ID-HAM either.

Additionally, we examine how well ID-HAM performs for real-time video broadcasts with varying mutation periods. **FFmpeg** [37] enables the recipient host to rebuild the 1441 frame video that was delivered. The **MSU perceptual video quality tool** [38] is used to compare the reconstructed video segments with the supplied video. Video Quality Metric (VQM), Structural Similarity (SSIM), and average Peak Signal to Noise Ratio (PSNR) are used to compare video quality in Table 2.3 [39]. PSNR determines the ratio between the highest potential signal strength and the distortion noise power that degrades video quality. Video degradation is defined in SSIM as a shift in the way structural information is perceived. VQM uses the discrete cosine transform by taking use of the visual perception feature. In comparison with PSNR and SSIM, a higher VQM number indicates lower video quality. It is evident that the values of VQM somewhat rise and

Table 2.3 Comparison of average PSNR (dB), SSIM and VQM with different mutation periods

Mutation period	PSNR(dB)	SSIM	VQM
No ID-HAM	38.1738	0.9664	2.6352
ID-HAM(15s)	38.0804	0.9658	2.6736
ID-HAM(10s)	37.4988	0.9652	2.8123
ID-HAM(5s)	37.0640	0.9638	2.8592

the levels of SSIM and PSNR significantly drop when the mutation time shortens. All of these findings clearly demonstrate that ID-HAM has a tolerable impact on video quality.

2.5 Conclusion

We have presented an ID-HAM system in this study. First, we create a seamless mutation method and build an MDP to explain the HAM mutation processes. Second, we provide a workable address block assignment based on SMT while taking into account various limitations. Infeasible actions shall be eliminated out of the MDP action space by resolving the restricted satisfaction issue. Third, in order to teach HAM how to learn from scanning habits, we create an advantage actor-critic algorithm. Lastly, we verify the efficacy of ID-HAM through a number of simulation tests and security assessments. In order to test various scanning technologies, we also put in place a proof-of-concept prototype system.

In order to assist packets holding vIP addresses in traversing different domains, we will examine in future work how to implement the ID-HAM scheme into the context of distributed SDN or software-defined wide-area networks (SD-WANs). Additionally, we will talk about how to easily adjust ID-HAM to more network scenarios.

References

1. Xu, C., Zhang, T., Kuang, X., Zhou, Z., Yu, S.: Context-aware adaptive route mutation scheme: a reinforcement learning approach. IEEE Internet Things J. **8**(17), 13528–13541 (2021)
2. Mazurczyk, W., Caviglione, L.: Cyber reconnaissance techniques. Commun. ACM **64**(3), 86–95 (2021)
3. Sun, J., Sun, K.: Desir: decoy-enhanced seamless ip randomization. In: Proceedings of 35th Annual IEEE International Conference on Computer Communications (INFOCOM), pp. 1–9 (2016)
4. Sharma, D.P., Kim, D.S., Yoon, S., Lim, H., Cho, J., Moore, T.J.: Frvm: flexible random virtual ip multiplexing in software-defined networks. In: Proceedings of 17th IEEE International Conference on Trust, Security and Privacy in Computing and Communications (TrustCom), pp. 579–587 (2018)

5. Yoon, S., Cho, J., Kim, D.S., Moore, T.J., Nelson, F., Lim, H.: Poster: address shuffling based moving target defense for in-vehicle software-defined networks. In: Proceedings of 25th Annual International Conference on Mobile Computing and Networking (Mobicom), pp. 1–3 (2019)
6. Narantuya, J., Yoon, S., Lim, H., Cho, J., Kim, D.S., Moore, T., Nelson, F.: Sdn-based ip shuffling moving target defense with multiple sdn controllers. In: Proceedings of 49th Annual IEEE/IFIP International Conference on Dependable Systems and Networks - Supplemental Volume (DSN-S), pp. 15–16 (2019)
7. Jafarian, J.H., Al-Shaer, E., Duan, Q.: An effective address mutation approach for disrupting reconnaissance attacks. IEEE Trans. Inf. Forensics Secur. **10**(12), 2562–2577 (2015)
8. Wang, S., Pei, Q., Wang, J., Tang, G., Zhang, Y., Liu, X.: An intelligent deployment policy for deception resources based on reinforcement learning. IEEE Access **8**, 35792–35804 (2020)
9. Xu, Q., Su, Z., Lu, R.: Game theory and reinforcement learning based secure edge caching in mobile social networks. IEEE Trans. Inf. Forensics Secur. **15**, 3415–3429 (2020)
10. Kim, J., Nam, J., Lee, S., Yegneswaran, V., Porras, P., Shin, S.: Bottlenet: hiding network bottlenecks using sdn-based topology deception. IEEE Trans. Inf. Forensics Secur. **16**, 3138–3153 (2021)
11. Zhou, Y., Cheng, G., Yu, S.: An sdn-enabled proactive defense framework for ddos mitigation in iot networks. IEEE Trans. Inf. Forensics Secur. **16**, 5366–5380 (2021)
12. Xing, J., Yang, M., Zhou, H., Wu, C., Ruan, W.: Hiding and trapping: a deceptive approach for defending against network reconnaissance with software-defined network. In: Proceedings of IEEE 38th International Performance Computing and Communications Conference (IPCCC), pp. 1–8 (2019)
13. Cho, J., Sharma, D.P., Alavizadeh, H., Yoon, S., Ben-Asher, N., Moore, T.J., Kim, D.S., Lim, H., Nelson, F.F.: Toward proactive, adaptive defense: a survey on moving target defense. IEEE Commun. Surv. Tutor. **22**(1), 709–745 (2020)
14. Zhou, Z., Kuang, X., Sun, L., Zhong, L., Xu, C.: Endogenous security defense against deductive attack: when artificial intelligence meets active defense for online service. IEEE Commun. Mag. **58**(6), 58–64 (2020)
15. Zhang, T., Kuang, X., Zhou, Z., Gao, H., Xu, C.: An intelligent route mutation mechanism against mixed attack based on security awareness. In: 2019 IEEE Global Communications Conference (GLOBECOM), pp. 1–6 (2019)
16. Achleitner, S., La Porta, T.F., McDaniel, P., Sugrim, S., Krishnamurthy, S.V., Chadha, R.: Deceiving network reconnaissance using sdn-based virtual topologies. IEEE Trans. Netw. Serv. Manag. **14**(4), 1098–1112 (2017)
17. Liu, Z., Wang, L.: Flipit game model-based defense strategy against cyberattacks on scada systems considering insider assistance. IEEE Trans. Inf. Forensics Secur. **16**, 2791–2804 (2021)
18. Nmap: the network mapper (2021). https://nmap.org/
19. Zheng, J., Namin, A.S.: A markov decision process to determine optimal policies in moving target. In: Proceedings of ACM SIGSAC Conference on Computer and Communications Security (CCS), Toronto, October 15–19, pp. 2321–2323 (2018)
20. Birkinshaw, C., Rouka, E., Vassilakis, V.G.: Implementing an intrusion detection and prevention system using software-defined networking: defending against port-scanning and denial-of-service attacks. J. Netw. Comput. Appl. **136**, 71–85 (2019)
21. Mishra, P., Varadharajan, V., Tupakula, U., Pilli, E.S.: A detailed investigation and analysis of using machine learning techniques for intrusion detection. IEEE Commun. Surv. Tutor. **21**(1), 686–728 (2019)
22. Anthi, E., Williams, L., Slowinska, M., Theodorakopoulos, G., Burnap, P.: A supervised intrusion detection system for smart home iot devices. IEEE Internet Things J. **6**(5), 9042–9053 (2019)
23. Moura, L.D., Bjørner, N.: Satisfiability modulo theories: introduction and applications. Commun. ACM **54**(9), 69–77 (2011)

References

24. Moura, L.D., Bjørner, N.: Z3: an efficient smt solver. In: Proceedings of the International Conference on Tools and Algorithms for the Construction and Analysis of Systems, pp. 337–340 (2008)
25. Liaskos, C., Ioannidis, S.: Network topology effects on the detectability of crossfire attacks. IEEE Trans. Inf. Forensics Secur. **13**(7), 1682–1695 (2018)
26. Mnih, V., Badia, A.P., Mirza, M., et al.: Asynchronous methods for deep reinforcement learning. In: Proceedings of the 33nd International Conference on Machine Learning (ICML), pp. 1928–1937 (2016)
27. Du, J., Yu, F.R., Lu, G., Wang, J., Jiang, J., Chu, X.: Mec-assisted immersive vr video streaming over terahertz wireless networks: a deep reinforcement learning approach. IEEE Internet Things J. **7**(10), 9517–9529 (2020)
28. Ryu sdn framework (2021). https://ryu-sdn.org/
29. Hagberg, A., Swart, P., Chult, D.S.: Exploring network structure, dynamics, and function using networkx. Technical report, Los Alamos National Laboratory (LANL), Los Alamos (2008)
30. Abadi, M., Barham, P., Chen, J., Chen, Z., et al.: Tensorflow: a system for large-scale machine learning. In: Proceedings of 12th USENIX Symposium on Operating Systems Design and Implementation (OSDI), pp. 265–283 (2016)
31. Dishington, C., Sharma, D.P., Kim, D.S., Cho, J., Moore, T.J., Nelson, F.F.: Security and performance assessment of ip multiplexing moving target defence in software defined networks. In: Proceedings of 18th IEEE International Conference on Trust, Security and Privacy in Computing and Communications (TrustCom), pp. 288–295 (2019)
32. Jafarian, J.H., Al-Shaer, E., Duan, Q.: Adversary-aware ip address randomization for proactive agility against sophisticated attackers. In: Proceedings of IEEE Conference on Computer Communications (INFOCOM), pp. 738–746 (2015)
33. arp-scan (2021). https://github.com/royhills/arp-scan
34. Fping (2021). https://fping.org/
35. Netdiscover (2021). https://github.com/alexxy/netdiscover
36. iperf: the tcp, udp and sctp network bandwidth measurement tool (2021). https://iperf.fr/
37. Ffmpeg (2021). https://www.ffmpeg.org/
38. Video filtering and compression by msu video group (cs msu graphics & media lab) (2021). https://www.compression.ru/video
39. Xu, C., Quan, W., Zhang, H., Grieco, L.A.: Grims: green information-centric multimedia streaming framework in vehicular ad hoc networks. IEEE Trans. Circuits Syst. Video Technol. **28**(2), 483–498 (2018)

Chapter 3
AI-Driven Moving Target Defense for DTMN: Collaborative Mutation-Based Moving Target Defense Based on Hierarchical Reinforcement Learning

Abstract As new IoT technologies evolve quickly, digital twins (DT) are being suggested for a number of uses. It is anticipated that DT and a mobile network would combine to create a DTMN. Nevertheless, DTMN is vulnerable to serious security risks, and the defenses in place are mostly inert and only react when an assault takes place. In this study, we present a collaborative mutation-based MTD (CM-MTD) for DTMN, which uses two techniques to modify network attributes and interrupt several stages of the cyber death chain: HAM and RM. We use a SMDP to represent dynamic deployment of MTD schemes and time-varying security events. LSTM predicts security occurrences and eliminates impractical activities from the action space. Lastly, we develop a deep reinforcement learning system for collaborative scheduling that is hierarchical. In comparison to baseline solutions, simulation results show how successful CM-MTD is.

Keywords Digital twins · Moving target defense · Attack prediction · Hierarchical deep reinforcement learning

3.1 Introduction

3.1.1 Motivations

By 2050, 24 billion physical devices, including wearable technology, cell phones, and electric cars, will be online. The IoT is the term utilized to describe the huge number of different physical objects that communicate to one another via heterogeneous (wired/wireless) communications [1]. Mobile networks are among the most significant network situations in the Internet of Things, and they have been around for a long time. However, the accelerated growth of DT is made possible by developing technologies in the IoT, such as 5G, AI, and SDN. The scale of the DT market will continue to grow in the future. Digital assets, which have uses in healthcare, aviation and manufacturing are used by DT to describe physical assets [2]. The network requirements for these DT applications are varied and stringent, including latency and QoS. The DTMN, which combines DT and mobile networks, is suggested as a solution to meet the above listed network criteria. This will enhance network performance and lower communication and computation costs.

There are three types of spaces in DT: digital, physical, and communication spaces that link the physical and digital spaces [3]. Bidirectional interfaces are provided by the communication space, meaning that digital assets manage information from physical assets and generate fresh data that may be sent back to the physical world. *DT for mobile networks* and *mobile networks for DT* are the two components of DTMN, as per the taxonomy in [4]. For the second case, security is crucial as cyber attacks may easily penetrate the communication space, causing DTMN to suffer significant harm [5]. Security concerns in DTMN have drawn an extensive amount of attention over the past few years. For instance, a safe autonomous system for intelligent manufacturing transportation was presented in the work in [6]. The efficiency of the aforementioned defense measures is severely limited since they typically react after attacks have occurred.

3.1.2 Challenges

In order to address the problem for "reactive response," MTD has been proposed as being a revolutionary method [7]. In order to prevent cyberattacks, MTD methods dynamically modify relevant network characteristics, such as IP addresses and transmission channels, to render the attackers' past knowledge invalid. Three significant issues still remain, nevertheless, when attempting to integrate MTD into DTMN. First off, while many MTD schemes are created to prevent a variety of attack types in mind, no single MTD scheme is able to fully secure DTMN. Few studies now take into account the cooperative scheduling of many MTD methods. Second, although deploying various MTD techniques continuously in DTMN may increase defensive efficacy, it will also incur significant network resource costs. The deployment time assignment of several MTD techniques to minimize the use of resources has seldom been the focus of prior efforts. Third, present MTD approaches do not take into account the future outcomes of attack-defend confrontations. Instead, they base their defensive judgments only on available information.

3.1.3 Contributions

We suggest a CM-MTD approach in DTMN to overcome the aforementioned issues. The two sample MTD techniques that we primarily examine in this work are RM and HAM. HAM and RM can function together since both techniques modify network characteristics while destroying separate parts of the cyber kill chain, such as network reconnaissance and attack execution. CM-MTD uses hierarchical deep

3.1 Introduction

reinforcement learning (HDRL) and attack prediction to dynamically organize the deployment of HAM and RM. Our earlier research [8–10] has demonstrated that DRL is a viable approach to greatly enhance MTD's defensive performance. Using the LSTM, CM-MTD forecasts the adversary's potential harmful actions. In the past few years, LSTM has become considered a standard method for handling sequences of time data and extracting short- and long-term information. The HDRL network state will then be the anticipated security incidents. In HDRL, the bottom layer learns from harmful actions to identify mutant routes or allocated IP address spaces, while the top layer determines the implementation type for MTD schemes. As far as we are aware, our study is the initial attempt to build an intelligent as well as cooperative MTD system in DTMN.

In conclusion, the following is a list of the paper's primary contributions in the amount:

1. To explain time-varying security incidents and the dynamic implementation of different MTD methods, we develop a SMDP model. In contrast to conventional MDP, SMDP can manage sequential decision-making and simulates the continuous-time discrete-event situation. Since security incidents are connected to incentives and action to be done, we construct network state as the jointly predicted security incidents of every network node, without depending just on current information. Furthermore, we characterize action as implementing relevant MTD schemes in accordance with the chosen macro-action, and macro-action as selecting the implementation strategy.
2. LSTM makes accurate predictions about the network status by using security logs to forecast future security incidents. Furthermore, the assignment of IP address spaces and the selection of modified routes are defined as constrained satisfaction problems using SMT, which takes into account a number of real-world network limitations, such as operation, flow table size, and QoS. The solution will be more effectively obtained by eliminating impractical actions from the SMDP action space by addressing the previously described restricted satisfaction issue.
3. We develop an HDRL method for collaborative scheduling based on the SMDP specifications, where the complexity of mutation activities may be decreased by hierarchical structure. Based on anticipated security events, macro-action in the upper layer determines the RM and/or HAM deployment category. According on the chosen macro-action, the bottom layer then selects allocated IP address spaces and/or altered routes on a regular basis. By using adaptive implementation of RM and HAM to learn from harmful behaviors, HDRL aims to increase protection performance and lower resource overheads.
4. To verify the efficacy of CM-MTD, a number of Mininet-WiFi simulations are run, covering prediction, defense, network, and convergence performances. In order to do examinations, we also put in place a proof-of-concept prototype system. In conclusion, our suggested CM-MTD can enhance defensive performance without having a negative effect on QoS when compared to baseline techniques.

3.1.4 Related Work

In an extensive variety of industries, for example manufacturing, healthcare, autonomous vehicles, smart cities, and more, DTMN applications have received an increasing amount of attention lately. However, both the conventional IoT and the new DTMN are vulnerable to attack by adversaries. According to the theory of the cyber kill chain, the two primary steps in breaching security objectives that seek to impair network performance are network reconnaissance and DDoS. Actually, several studies have concentrated on DDoS and network reconnaissance in the IoT. For example, I. Cvitic et al. [11] created a logistic tree-based traffic detection technique for various IoT devices in order to protect against DDoS. At the same time, DT security must be safeguarded from cyberattacks. A safe autonomous system for intelligent manufacturing transportation was presented in the work in [6]. Nevertheless, practically all of the above stated techniques as well as other security plans now in use are reactive, meaning that before defense measures start working, the network system has already been infiltrated for a while and has suffered serious harm.

Luckily, MTD has being used to address this significant issue. To protect against DDoS and network reconnaissance, respectively, two MTD schemes were developed: RM and HAM [7]. RM periodically modifies communication paths to prevent connections and nodes attacked by DDoS. And HAM periodically modifies IP addresses to enhance the variety, complexity, and randomization of end-hosts. It was suggested by Sharma et al. [12, 13] to transform actual IP addresses into time-varying, random virtual IP addresses. H. Wang et al. [14] created an adaptive mutation period RM scheme. An intelligent RM method based on DRL was introduced in the work in [15].

Since DTMN has a complicated network situation and a variety of network requirements, a single MTD scheme cannot provide full protection for DTMN, even though MTD solutions greatly improve defensive performance. In reality, RM prevents connections or nodes from being compromised by DDoS, whereas HAM disrupts the information gathering process of network reconnaissance. They thereby render several steps of the cyber kill chain invalid. Consequently, RM and HAM could work in tandem to provide more robust security. The collaboration between several MTD methods has not been thoroughly studied before. Furthermore, HAM and RM's continuing deployment will need a lot of network resources. For the first time, the CM-MTD strategy utilizing threat prediction and HDRL is proposed in this contribution to close these gaps.

3.2 Model Formulation on the Edge Layer

We provide the introduction of network, threat, and SMDP models in this section.

3.2 Model Formulation on the Edge Layer

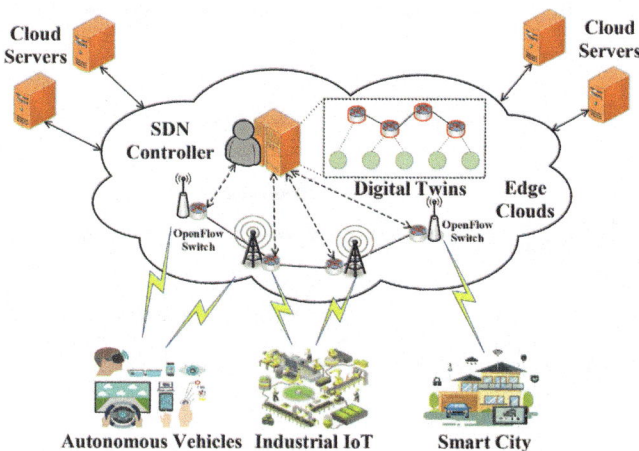

Fig. 3.1 The architecture of SDN-IoT in DTMN

3.2.1 Network Model

The SDN-IoT architecture in DTMN is shown in Fig. 3.1. Massively diverse sensors that enable a an extensive variety of applications, for example driverless cars, industrial IoT, and smart cities, and distant cloud servers that offer Internet access make up the physical device layer. OpenFlow switches are housed in RSUs and base stations (BSs). And these BSs and RSUs serve as routers for cloud servers and points of entry for mobile devices or stationary such as sensors and cars. SDN controllers are situated on edge servers, which make up the control layer. Network visualization, security optimization, and other applications are implemented via the DT layer.

An undirected graph $\mathcal{G} = \{\mathcal{V}, \mathcal{M}, \mathcal{E}\}$ can be used to model the SDN-IoT in DTMN. Here, $\mathcal{V}$ represents the collection of cloud nodes and IoT devices v_i^n ($1 \leq i \leq n$), $\mathcal{M}$ represents the collection of OpenFlow switches v_j^s ($1 \leq j \leq m$), and $\mathcal{E}$ represents the collection of wired/wireless links connecting various switches and/or nodes. sensors, vehicles and Cloud servers are all regarded as terminals in the context of edge clouds.

3.2.2 Threat Model

Remote cloud servers in DTMN offer Internet services for a range of DT applications, making them vulnerable to attack. However, extensive security measures cannot be implemented because of the limited resources of large IoT devices. As a result, a great deal of IoT devices can be readily entered by an attacker and turned

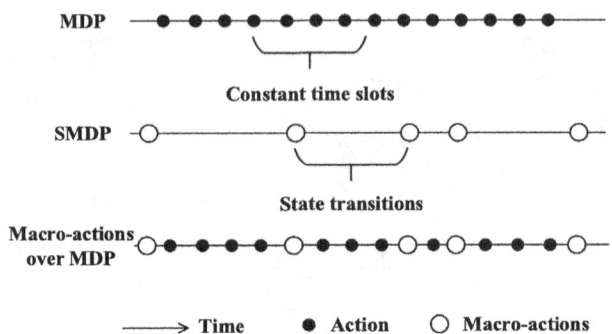

Fig. 3.2 The state trajectories of MDP and SMDP

into a botnet. The attacker then uses the botnet to perform cyberattacks against cloud services, causing network disruption or even paralysis.

Depending on the cyber kill chain, the attacker often employs a multi-phase attack that includes both the reconnaissance phase such as port and IP scanning and attack stage of execution such as DDoS flooding [16]. Furthermore, we presume that the enemy is logical and has a small botnet to initiate cyberattacks [17]. The attack execution phase often lasts for a few hours or days before moving on to the subsequent reconnaissance phase.

3.2.3 Semi-Markov Decision Process Model

Given that sequential decision-making is a feature of collaborative scheduling, we construct the dynamic deploying of different MTD methods as an SMDP model, as seen in Fig. 3.2. The open circle in the SMDP's upper layer denotes the macro-action pertaining to the first decision of whether to deploy HAM or RM. Time is separated into equal slots in the lowest layer of SMDP, which are represented by the symbol Δt. The solid black dot indicates that IP address spaces are assigned and/or modified routes are selected according to macro-action. When macro-actions alter, further actions are carried out, allowing the higher and lower levels to interact via reward feedback.

3.2.3.1 Network State Space

The security events for every network node inside the DTMN are referred to as the network state. The vector $S_t = \{e_1^{t+1}, e_2^{t+1}, \cdots, e_n^{t+1}\}$ represents the network state, where e_i^{t+1} represents the anticipated security event at the time period v_i^n ($1 \leq i \leq n$) at time slot $t + 1$. Section 3.3.2.1 will introduce LSTM, which is used to forecast future security incidents of network nodes. The overall amount of network states is

3.2 Model Formulation on the Edge Layer

going to be $\Gamma = L^n$ where there are L potential security incidents. For this reason, $\{S_1, \cdots, S_\Gamma\}$ is used to characterize network state space.

3.2.3.2 Action Space

The two steps involved in our MTD systems in this research are (1) allocating IP address spaces to network nodes and (2) choosing mutant routes for flows. The multi-dimensional vector $A_t = \{\mathbb{I}_t, \mathbb{B}_t\}$ represents collaborative mutation, where $\mathbb{I}_t = \{I_{1,1}, \cdots, I_{i,x}, \cdots, I_{n,w}\}$ and $\mathbb{B}_t = \{B_1^{f_1}, \cdots, B_m^{f_1}, \cdots, B_1^{f_k}, \cdots, B_m^{f_k}\}$. If node v_i^n is given x-th IP address space, then $I_{i,x}$ ($1 \leq i \leq n, 1 \leq x \leq w$) equals 1; if not, $I_{i,x} = 0$. If the OpenFlow switch v_j^s is chosen to be in the path of flow f_y, the value of $B_j^{f_y}$ ($1 \leq j \leq m, 1 \leq y \leq k$) equals 1; if not, $B_j^{f_y} = 0$. All conceivable actions make up the action space, which we call as $\mathcal{A}$. Section 3.3.1 formalizes the many network limitations that must be met by the majority of operations in the aforementioned space.

3.2.3.3 Macro-Action Space

The generalization of activities is referred to as macro-actions. This study defines the macro-action space as $O = \{o_c, o_a, o_r, o_s\}$. The o_c indicates both HAM and RM deployment, o_a indicates just HAM deployment, o_r indicates only RM deployment, and o_s indicates static IP addresses and routes. With $\mathcal{I}$ as the initialization set, π as the action strategy, and ζ as the end condition, $<\mathcal{I}, \pi, \zeta>$ represents any $o \in O$. Policy π will determine which macro-actions are possible if $S_t \in \mathcal{I}$. In our network situation, the SDN controller has a capacity to adopt the chosen policy and decide the macro-action at each network state. Any macro-action has a termination condition ζ that occurs after constant time slots.

3.2.3.4 State Transitions

The shifting of anticipated security events will be considered a state transition accordance to the concept of network condition.

3.2.3.5 Reward Function

When the action is decided, prizes will be received. There are two elements to reward: (1) reward for defense R_d; (2) reward for resource consumption R_c. Evaluating the defensive efficacy is the goal of reward R_d, which is described as follows.

$$R_d = \begin{cases} -\alpha_1 \sum_{i \in n} \Theta_{t,i} - \alpha_2 \Upsilon_t, & \text{if attacks are successful,} \\ C, & \text{otherwise,} \end{cases} \quad (3.1)$$

In this context, α_1 and α_2 represent coefficients, $\Theta_{t,i}$ denotes the count of successful scans for node v_i^n during time slot t, Υ_t indicates the number of OpenFlow switches compromised by the attackers at time period t, and C serves as a positive value. The resource consume brought on by RM and/or HAM is assessed using reward R_c, which can be defined as follows:

$$R_c = \begin{cases} W_t, & \text{if macro-action is one of } o_c, o_a \text{ and } o_r, \\ 0, & \text{otherwise,} \end{cases} \quad (3.2)$$

In this context, the resource consumption function, W_t, can be defined as follows: $W_t = -\gamma_1 \sum_{i \in n} e_i^a - \gamma_2 \sum_{x \in k} e_x^r$. e_i^a indicates the resource consuming of HAM for network node v_i^n, e_y^r indicates the resource consuming for RM on flow f_y, and γ_1 and γ_2 are coefficients. Consequently, the whole prize is represented as follows:

$$R_{total} = R_d + R_c, \quad (3.3)$$

where the incentive of the macro-action is a combined amount of the incentive from the selected activities, and R_{total} is computed after each action.

3.3 Detailed Design

We designed a CM-MTD system that automatically modifies the duration of deployment allotment of RM and HAM to protect against multi-step attacks. HAM regularly changes the IP addresses of network nodes to thwart enemy reconnaissance. However, in an effort to lessen DDoS damage, RM regularly modifies routes to steer clear of OpenFlow switches that have been attacked by DDoS. The execution techniques of RM and HAM have been presented in current works [12–15], and consequently, we get rid of their detail for brevity.

Our suggested CM-MTD scheme's framework is displayed in Fig. 3.3. Security events are produced at the physical device layer by the detection logs of network nodes, such as cloud servers and IoT devices. Existing security techniques, such as intrusion detection systems and firewalls, have the ability of detecting different stages of attacks. The LSTM, which seeks to forecast future security events of network nodes, will then use these security events as input (details are provided in Sect. 3.3.2.1). The action space of SMDP will be cleared of impractical activities that fail to meet certain network limitations (details in Sect. 3.3.1). Lastly, HDRL will use the results of SMT formalization and LSTM as the network action and state, in each case. Iteratively updating can be used to determine the best strategy for deploying RM and/or HAM (details are provided in Sect. 3.3.2.2).

3.3 Detailed Design

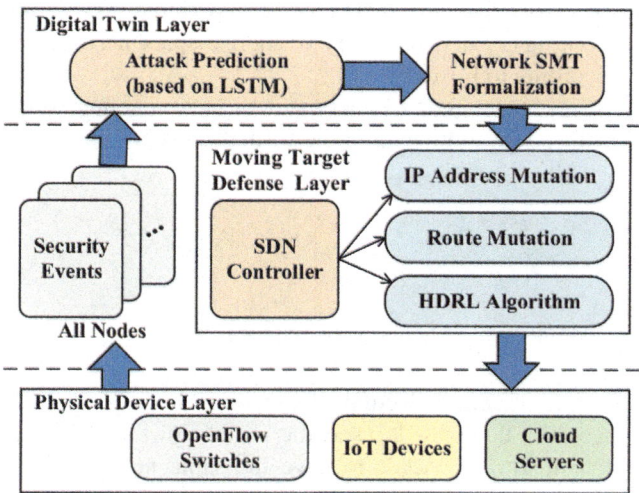

Fig. 3.3 The framework of our proposed CM-MTD scheme

3.3.1 Collaborative Mutation Formalization

We use SMT to formalize the issue of choosing modified routes and allocating IP address spaces as a restricted satisfaction problem in this subsection. Whether IP address space z_x is allocated to network node v_i^n is indicated by the binary variable b_i^x. In that case, $b_i^x = 1$; if not, $b_i^x = 0$. The binary variable d_j^y indicates if the OpenFlow switch v_j^s is chosen to be a part of the flow f_y's path. In that case, $d_j^y = 1$; if not, $d_j^y = 0$. The conceivable operations of HAM and RM should meet certain network limitations while taking into account actual network circumstances.

3.3.1.1 Operation Constraints

Basic network operating restrictions must be met via collaborative mutation. The following is a formalization of the restrictions on IP address space assignment:

$$\sum_{x=1}^{w} b_i^x \geq 1, \forall v_i^n \in \mathcal{V}, \quad (3.4)$$

$$\sum_{i=1}^{n} b_i^x = 1, \forall x \in [1, w], \quad (3.5)$$

The total amount of IP address spaces allotted to a single node is higher than or equal to one, according to Eq. (3.4). Every IP address space needs to be allocated to a single node, according to Eq. (3.5).

Every flow f_y ($1 \leq y \leq k$) is assumed to have a source switch s_y and a destination switch d_y. The following is the formalization of an acceptable altered route of flow f_x with accessible restrictions.

$$\sum_{e_j \in \mathbb{O}_j} d_j^y = \sum_{e_j \in \mathbb{P}_j} d_j^y, \forall v_j^s \in \mathcal{V}, \forall f_y \in \mathcal{F}, \tag{3.6}$$

$$d_j^y \in \{0, 1\}, \forall v_j^s \in \mathcal{V}, \forall f_y \in \mathcal{F}, \tag{3.7}$$

In OpenFlow switch v_j^s, the collection of outgoing flows is denoted by $\mathbb{O}_j$, the collection of incoming flows by $\mathbb{P}_j$, and the set of flows is denoted by $\mathcal{F}$. Each OpenFlow switch in flow f_y needs to have the same number of incoming and outgoing flows, according to Eq. (3.6). The numerical value range of the variable d_j^y is defined by Eq. (3.7).

3.3.1.2 Flow Table Size Constraint

OpenFlow switches' flow tables need to be updated to reflect changes in the IP address spaces allotted to various network nodes. Supernetting is going to be used to combine nearby IP address spaces into bigger ones if they are assigned to the same network node. This can help to minimize the size of the flow table. The binary variable $\mathcal{D}_{x_1,x_2}$ indicates either IP address spaces z_{x_1} and z_{x_2} are nonadjacent, assuming this. $\mathcal{D}_{x_1,x_2} = 1$ if it is the case, and $\mathcal{D}_{x_1,x_2} = 0$ otherwise. Then, whether nonadjacent IP address spaces z_{x_1} and z_{x_2} are allocated to the same network node v_i^n is indicated by the binary variable $\mathcal{L}_i^{x_1,x_2}$. The following formula determines the value of $\mathcal{L}_i^{x_1,x_2}$:

$$\mathcal{L}_i^{x_1,x_2} = b_i^{x_1} \wedge b_i^{x_2} \wedge \mathcal{D}_{x_1,x_2}. \tag{3.8}$$

The flow table will have fewer entries available if more flows go via the OpenFlow switch v_i^s. OpenFlow switches are unable to execute lookups in a timely manner when the flow table size becomes big. the flow size of the table restriction is expressed as follows:

$$\sum_{x_1=1}^{m} \sum_{x_2 \neq x_1} \sum_{i \in l_j^y} \mathcal{L}_i^{x_1,x_2} + \sum_{y=1}^{k} \sum_{j \in r_y} d_j^y \leq \mathbb{C}_j^{cap}, \forall f_y \in \mathcal{F}, \tag{3.9}$$

Here, l_j^y represents the network nodes linked to OpenFlow switch v_j^s, which acts as either the source or destination switch for flow f_y. Meanwhile, r_y refers to the

3.3 Detailed Design

OpenFlow switches along the transmission route of flow f_y, excluding the source and destination switches, and $\mathbb{C}_j^{cap}$ indicates the maximum capacity of the flow table for OpenFlow switch v_j^s.

3.3.1.3 Quality of Service Constraint

The various QoS of DTMN, including maximum hops and transmission latency, should be satisfied via collaborative mutation. The following is the formalization of the QoS constraint:

$$\sum_{j=1}^{m} d_j^y T_j^m + \sum_{j_1=1}^{m} \sum_{j_2 \neq j_1} d_{j_1}^y d_{j_2}^y T_l \leq \mathbb{C}_y^{del}, \tag{3.10}$$

With T_l representing the link delay, $\mathbb{C}_y^{del}$ representing the longest possible delay limit for flow f_y, while T_j^m representing the processing delay resulting from changing the packets' IP address if v_j^s is the source or target switch. Otherwise, lookups will cause T_j^m to be forward delayed if v_j^s is the intermediate switch.

3.3.2 Intelligent Collaborative Mutation Scheme

We first describe the way to use LSTM for assault prediction in this paragraph. Next, in order to determine the dynamic employment of several MTD methods, we create a new HDRL algorithm.

3.3.2.1 Long Short-Term Memory for Attack Prediction

In order to forecast attack kinds and targets for a future time slot, attack prediction uses event sequences from past collections. LSTM has come to be as an acceptable method for handling time series information in recent years. LSTM and HDRL may be closely integrated as the final stage of LSTM will serve as the initial layer of HDRL. In the realm of MTD, LSTM is rarely used to increase HDRL's macro-action efficiency.

Detection logs are used to create security events. The equation $E_i = \{e_i^1, e_i^2, \cdots, e_i^t\}$ represents the arrival of the security incident sequence for network node v_i^n. The formula for the arrival sequence of security events for every network node is $\mathbb{E} = \{E_1, E_2, \cdots, E_n\}^T$. The neural network of attack prediction is then constructed using $\phi(\mathbf{X}_p; \theta_p)$, where $\mathbf{X}_p$ represents the input and θ_p represents the neural network's parameters. The security event sequence training data is represented as follows:

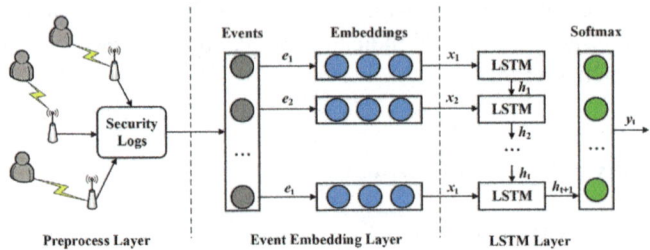

Fig. 3.4 Security logs are collected and extracted to events in preprocess layer, then put into event embedding layer to construct the context-based representation. Finally, LSTM is used to predict the future security event

$$[X \mid Y] = \begin{bmatrix} E_k^1 & E_k^2 & \cdots & E_k^L & E_k^{L+1} \\ E_k^2 & E_k^3 & \cdots & E_k^{L+1} & E_k^{L+2} \\ & & \vdots & & \vdots \\ E_k^{t-L} & E_k^{t-L+1} & \cdots & E_k^{t-1} & E_k^t \end{bmatrix}, \quad (3.11)$$

Here, $k \in 1, 2, \cdots, n$, E_k^t represents the security event gathered by network node v_i^n during time slot t, $X_k^t = E_k^{t-L}, E_k^{t-L+1}, \cdots, E_k^{t-1}$, $Y_k^t = E_k^t$, and each row corresponds to a sample data point.

The complete architecture of assault prediction using the LSTM network (LSTMNet) is shown in Fig. 3.4. Security logs are used to produce a number of characteristics in the preprocess layer, including node ID, timestamp, event description, and security event ID. Security incidents are mapped into the lower dimensionality space in the event embedding layer [16]. LSTMNet will be developed in the LSTM layer to achieve high attack prediction accuracy. The likelihood distribution of future safety occurrences is obtained by adding the Softmax function. Mean square error is used by the loss function to quantify the difference between actual and expected data. Lastly, the loss function is minimized using an adaptive optimizer named Adam [18].

3.3.2.2 Hierarchical Deep Reinforcement Learning for Collaborative Mutation

We develop a new HDRL method for collaborative mutation in this subsubsection. As seen in Fig. 3.5, the bottom layer uses PPO [19] to figure out the optimum strategy for choosing mutation actions, while the top layer uses DQN [20] to achieve the best strategy of deployment choices. LSTMNet, which forecasts future security incidents, will produce the network state. Actually, depending on the real-world scenario, the total amount of collectively projected network nodes may be dynamically decided. This is due to LSTMNet's low complexity when fewer

3.3 Detailed Design

Algorithm 2 Hierarchical deep reinforcement learning for collaborative mutation

1: Set parameters ε and α in DQN;
2: Set parameters ξ, ϵ, and γ in PPO;
3: Set batch size T and minibatch size K;
4: Initialize experience replay buffer $\mathcal{B}_1 = \varnothing$, $\mathcal{B}_2 = \varnothing$;
5: Initialize main Q-network with weight θ_t^u;
6: Initialize target Q-network with weight $\theta_{t-n}^u = \theta_t^u$;
7: Initialize critic network $V(S_k, \phi)$;
8: Initialize actor network with weight θ_k^l;
9: **for** $episode = 1, 2, \cdots, M$ **do**
10:    **for** $t = 1, 2, \cdots, T$ **do**
11:       Obtain current state S_t by LSTMNet;
12:       Generate a random probability p;
13:       Select macro-action O_t as,
14:       **if** $p \leq \varepsilon$ **then**
15:          Select a macro-action O_t randomly;
16:       **else**
17:          $O_t = \arg\max_{O'} Q_t(S_t, O_t; \theta_t^u)$;
18:       **end if**
19:       **for** $k = 1, 2, \cdots, K$ **do**
20:          Run policy $\pi_{\theta_{k-n}^l}$ to select action A_k;
21:          Deploy corresponding MTD schemes;
22:          Observe lower layer reward R_k^l;
23:          Collect $\mathcal{D}_k = (S_k, A_k, R_k^l, S_{k+1})$;
24:          Store into the replay buffer $\mathcal{B}_2 = \mathcal{B}_2 \cup \mathcal{D}_k$;
25:          Calculate TD errors δ_t;
26:          $\hat{A}_k = \sum_{q=k}^{K} (\gamma\xi)^{q-k} \delta_q$;
27:          Estimate value target $\hat{V}_k = \hat{A}_k + V(S_k, \phi)$;
28:       **end for**
29:       Observe upper layer reward R_t^u;
30:       Obtain next state S_{t+1} by LSTMNet;
31:       Collect $\mathcal{D}_t' = \{S_t, O_t, R_t^u, S_{t+1}\}$;
32:       Store into the replay buffer $\mathcal{B}_1 = \mathcal{B}_1 \cup \mathcal{D}_t'$;
33:    **end for**
34:    **for** $epoch = 1, 2, \cdots, U$ **do**
35:       Calculate the target Q-value y_t;
36:       Minimize the loss function by gradient descent;
37:       $\mathcal{J}^{actor}(\theta) = \frac{1}{K}\sum_{k=1}^{K} \min(r_k(\theta), clip(r_k(\theta), 1-\epsilon, 1+\epsilon))\hat{A}_k$;
38:       Update θ_k^l by $\nabla_\theta \mathcal{J}^{actor}$;
39:       $\mathcal{J}^{critic}(\theta) = -\frac{1}{K}\sum_{k=1}^{K}(\hat{V}_k - V(S_k, \phi))^2$;
40:       Update ϕ by $\nabla_\phi \mathcal{J}^{critic}$;
41:    **end for**
42:    $\theta_{t-n}^u \leftarrow \theta_t^u$;
43:    $\theta_{k-n}^l \leftarrow \theta_k^l$;
44: **end for**

Fig. 3.5 The flowchart of our proposed HDRL algorithm

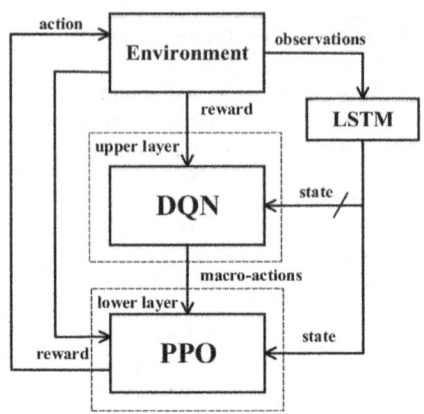

network nodes are anticipated independently. However, LSTMNet has a higher global accuracy when more network nodes are anticipated collectively.

Algorithm 5 displays the pseudo-code of our HDRL for collaborative mutation. First, the replay buffer, parameters, and DNNs are initialized (lines 1–8). In DQN, α represents the learning rate and ε represents the greedy factor. γ is the discount factor between 0 and 1 in PPO, ϵ is the parameter to regulate the clip range, and ξ is utilized to balance the tradeoff between variance and bias. There are primarily two loop sections in Algorithm 5 (line 9). Iteratively obtaining state-action samples is explained in the first section (lines 10–33). LSTMNet will retrieve the network state on each time slot (line 11). The ε-greedy approach will next be used to determine the macro-action (lines 12–18). PPO in the lower layer will choose the mutation actions after choosing a macro-action (lines 19–28). The SDN controller uses policy $\pi_{\theta_{k-n}^l}$ to select an action for deploying MTD schemes and then observes the lower-layer reward impacted by cyberattacks (lines 20–22). The state-action sample is kept in $\mathcal{B}_2$, the replay buffer. The advantage and value functions are then estimated, respectively, using the generalized advantage method of estimation (lines 24–27). The SDN controller will get the upper layer reward and the subsequent network state from LSTMNet once K iterations in the bottom layer are complete (lines 29–30). The replay buffer $\mathcal{B}_1$ contains the state and macro-action sample (lines 31–32). How to learn from samples is covered in the second section. The gradient descent approach is used in DQN to minimize the loss function (lines 35–36). The value function and policy gradient are computed in PPO, respectively. Furthermore, different parameters are updated appropriately (lines 37–40). Lastly, lines 42–43 will be altered for macro-action and action policy, respectively.

3.4 Performance Evaluation and Analysis

We carry out a number of simulations and put a prototype system into use to show the efficacy of our suggested CM-MTD scheme. We examine the prediction, defense, network, and convergence capabilities of the CM-MTD scheme.

3.4 Performance Evaluation and Analysis

Table 3.1 Simulation parameters

Parameter	Value or range
Parameters of Waxman model	$\alpha = 0.2, \beta = 0.15$
Number of OpenFlow switches	[12, 100]
Number of IoT devices	[10, 90]
Number of cloud servers	[2, 10]
Number of IP address spaces	[30, 150]
Communication range of OpenFlow switches	250 m
Link bandwidth	5 Mbps
Size of IP address space	128
Number of episodes in upper layer	10,000
Number of steps on each episode	25
Mini-batch size	5
GAE parameters	$\gamma = 0.99, \lambda = 0.95$
Clip coefficient in PPO	0.2
Hidden layers of DQN in the upper layer	[256]
Activation function	$ReLU$
Learning rate in DQN	10^{-3}
Hidden layers of PPO in the lower layer	[256, 256]
Activation function	$tanh$
Learning rate in PPO	10^{-4}
Learning optimizer	Adam

First, we used Mininet-WiFi [21], a wireless network simulator, to build CM-MTD with version 2.5. We then used Ryu 4.34 [22] as the SDN controller. The network architecture in our simulations is made up of 12/100 network nodes and 12/100 OpenFlow switches. The network topology is generated using the Waxman framework with the variables $\alpha = 0.2$ and $\beta = 0.15$ using Networkx 2.5 [23]. Certain parameter values have been shown to provide excellent training performance [24, 25]. For instance, the clip coefficient in PPO is 0.2, the learning optimizer uses Adam, and the GAE variables are set to $\gamma = 0.99$ and $\lambda = 0.95$. DQN and PPO have activation functions of $ReLU$ and $tanh$, correspondingly. Furthermore, we modify some parameter values according to the DTMN situation. For instance, the bottom layer's hidden levels of PPO are set to [256, 256], while the higher layer's hidden layers of DQN are set to [256]. Table 3.1 displays the simulation parameters.

3.4.1 Prediction Performance

The event chain produced by typical strategies for attack and the actual-world CICIDS-2017 [26] are used to test attacks prediction. Sequential scanning and direct DDoS are two methods of attacks used in event sequence generation [27].

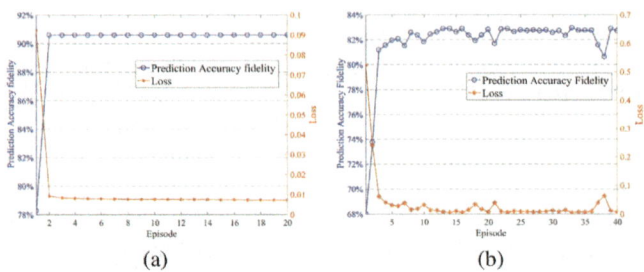

Fig. 3.6 The prediction accuracy fidelity and loss of attack prediction. (**a**) DDoS and sequential scanning. (**b**) CICIDS-2017

Benign and anomalous network traffic recorded over a five-day period is included in CICIDS-2017. The attacker is more probable to target network nodes having a high node level when launching direct DDoS attacks. Sequential scanning involves the adversary sending several probing queries in scanning area and then randomly reselecting the starting IP address over time. Thus, we primarily concentrate upon three categories of security incidents: DoS/DDoS, benign and infiltration. We use forecast fidelity as the parameter to assess attack prediction efficacy, and the results are shown as follows:

$$Fidelity = \frac{\sum_{i \in N} \mathbb{Y}(p_i, y_i)}{|N|}, \quad (3.12)$$

where $|N|$ is the total amount of safety incidents that occur on each of the network nodes, p_i is the projected security incident of network node v_i, and y_i is the real security incident of network node v_i. The forecast security event p_i and the actual security event y_i are equivalent if $\mathbb{Y}(p_i, y_i)$ equals 1. Its value is identical to 0 else. Additionally, we utilize 80% of the dataset for the training set and 20% as the testing set.

The prediction fidelity, accuracy and loss of CM-MTD in the event sequences produced by sequence scanning and DDoS are shown in Fig. 3.6a. While the loss drops from 0.09 to 0, the prediction accuracy fidelity quickly increases from 78% to 92%. The results of the simulation in Fig. 3.6b demonstrate that the prediction accuracy fidelity of CM-MTD comes together from 68% to 83% within 10 episodes under the event sequence produced by CICIDS-2017. At the same time, the CM-MTD loss drops from 0.5 to 0, signifying that the training is over. Because the incidence of harmful actions is not always regular, it is challenging to anticipate the real-world dataset CICIDS-2017 through contrasting simulator outcomes in two event series.

We assess confusion matrices on sets of testing under two incident sequences, respectively. The findings are shown in Fig. 3.7a, b. We also compute the prediction recall, accuracy and F1-score of two event sequences according to two confusion matrices. DoS/DDoS has the best forecast accuracy, whereas infiltration has the

3.4 Performance Evaluation and Analysis

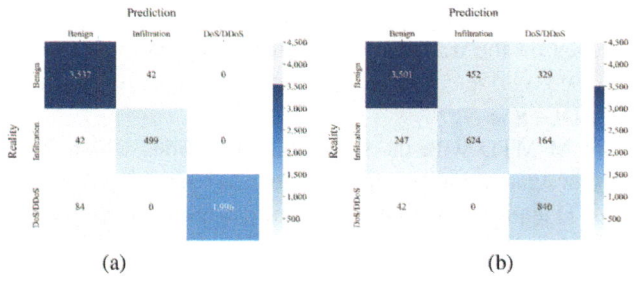

Fig. 3.7 The confusion matrix on the testing set. (**a**) DDoS and sequential scanning. (**b**) CICIDS-2017

Table 3.2 Simulation results

Event sequence	Type	Prediction accuracy	Recall	F1-score
DDoS and sequential scanning	Benign	96.56%	98.83%	97.68%
	Infiltration	92.24%	92.24%	92.24%
	DoS/DDoS	100%	95.56%	97.94%
CICIDS-2017	Benign	83.33%	92.37%	87.62%
	Infiltration	60.29%	57.99%	59.12%
	DoS/DDoS	95.24%	63.02%	75.85%

lowest, as seen by Fig. 3.7a, b, and Table 3.2. This is due to the fact that DoS/DDoS typically persists for a duration that may be effectively anticipated under DDoS+sequential scanning or CICIDS-2017. Conversely, infiltration, such as IP scanning, occurs in between harmless traffic and is not constant. As a result, infiltration is hard to forecast. For the same reason, benign has the highest F1-score and recall, whereas infiltration has the lowest F1-score and recall. According to simulation data, our suggested CM-MTD has a high degree of accuracy in forecasting future security occurrences.

3.4.2 Defense Performance

In the following subsection, we additionally assess the defensive performance with a real-world dataset, CICIDS-2017 [26], and two event sequences produced by realistic attack tactics. defensive success ratio (DSR), a statistic used to assess defensive performance, is represented as follows:

$$DSR = (1 - \frac{\sum_{k=1}^{n} N_k^s + \sum_{k=1}^{m} N_k^d}{\sum_{k=1}^{n} L_k^s + \sum_{k=1}^{m} L_k^d}) \times 100\%, \quad (3.13)$$

where the total amount of scanned network nodes is L_k^s, the total amount of OpenFlow switches on the transmission route is L_k^d, the total amount of network nodes compromised via scanning is N_k^s, and the count of OpenFlow switches compromised by DDoS is N_k^d.

We compare CM-MTD with the subsequent baselines which may be modified and used to protect against multi-step coordination assaults, given that our work is the first smart MTD approach with the dynamic planning and combined deployment of HAM and RM.

1. RRT [14]+ FRVM [12, 13]: RRT uses an adaptive mutation period to carry out the RM, making it appropriate for DDoS defense. For network scanning, FRVM transforms genuine IP addresses into time-varying, random virtual IP addresses. We simultaneously deploy FRVM and RRT as a baseline.
2. DQ-RM [15]+FRVM [12, 13]: The most advanced RM technique that dynamically modifies routes based on DRL is called DQ-RM. We also simultaneously deploy FRVM and DQ-RM as a baseline.

We create two attack series utilizing sequential scanning + direct DDoS [27] and sequential scanning + crossfire DDoS [28] in order to efficiently assess the defensive performance. The attacker is more probable to undertake a direct DDoS attack against highly ranked network nodes. The adversary first chooses a targeted region for crossfire DDoS, after which they transmit malicious traffic to neighboring nodes, causing shared connections to be throttled and indirectly leading to hacked nodes in the targeted area. Serial scanning involves the adversary sending several probing queries in scanning space and then randomly reselecting its starting IP address over time. While RRT+FRVM, CM-MTD and DQ-RM+FRVM are deployed, we compute average DSRs for every 1000 episodes. The following data show the average evaluation findings over 5 simulation runs. Furthermore, the evaluation findings' standard errors are displayed as error shadows.

The mean DSRs of CM-MTD are the highest in the three algorithms, convergent to 98.2% and 97%, each, as demonstrated in Fig. 3.8a, b. The rationale is that by learning from harmful activities, CM-MTD can improve the choice of allocated IP address spaces and modified routes. Due to DQ-RM selects mutant routes according to DQN and somewhat enhances defensive performance, the mean DSR of DQ-RM+FRVM converges from 90.5% to 92%. Conversely, due to RRT+FRVM uses a random mutation approach, its DSR remains constant over episodes. The mean DSR of CM-MTD converges from 89% to 95% through learning from attack traces in CICIDS-2017, according to simulation findings in Fig. 3.8c. The mean DSRs of RRT+FRVM and DQ-RM+FRVM are around 83% and 87%, respectively, which are lower than those of CM-MTD for the same reasons shown in Fig. 3.8a, b. Defense performance under various assault event sequences is compared in Fig. 3.8d. When CM-MTD is subjected to direct DDoS, its average convergence DSR is 98.2%, but when it is subjected to CICIDS-2017, it is only 95%. This is due to the difficulty of learning attack traces in CICIDS-2017. In conclusion, CM-MTD outperforms typical solutions in terms of defensive performance across two assault sequences and a real-life dataset.

3.4 Performance Evaluation and Analysis

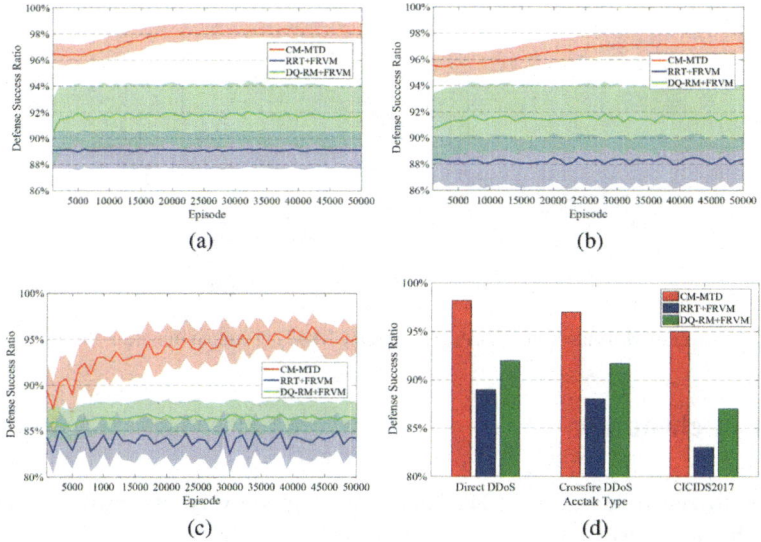

Fig. 3.8 Defense performance comparison while CM-MTD, RRT+FRVM, and DQ-RM+FRVM are deployed respectively. (**a**) Defense performance under direct DDoS and sequential scanning. (**b**) Defense performance under crossfire DDoS and sequential scanning. (**c**) Defense performance under CICIDS-2017. (**d**) Defense performance under different attack types

3.4.3 Network Performance

We use two metrics, PLR and RTT, which are calculated by iPerf 2.0.10 [29], to assess network performance. PLR is the percentage of packets out of all those created that are not received by the destinations. The RTT among the source and the destination is its definition.

When CM-MTD and no mutation are applied, we analyze the mean RTT and PLR with 300 s. The rate at which packets are sent is set at 9 Mbit/s. The average RTT of CM-MTD is typically between 2 and 4 ms, whereas the RTT of no mutation is around 1 ms, as seen in Fig. 3.9a. The abrupt rise in RTT is caused by CM-MTD's dynamic adjustment of allocated IP address spaces and/or modified routes. According to the simulation findings in Fig. 3.9b, the mean PLR of CM-MTD is often 0%, although occasionally it increases due to RM and HAM. Given that CM-MTD automatically modifies the time required to deploy the allotment of RM and HAM, it can be said that it only has a little impact on network performance. CM-MTD can shorten deployment times compared to constantly installing RM and HAM, which can lower network overheads brought on by MTD execution.

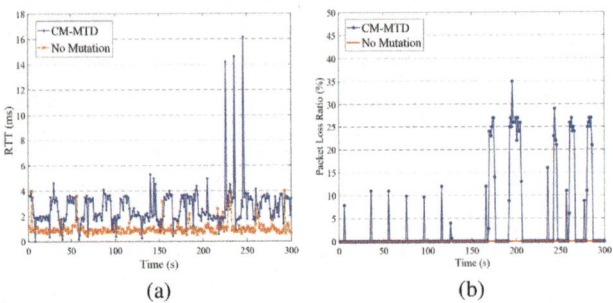

Fig. 3.9 Network performance comparison between CM-MTD and no mutation. (**a**) RTT. (**b**) PLR

3.5 Conclusion

In order to schedule several MTD methods cooperatively, we provide the CM-MTD scheme in this study. First, we use an SMDP model to represent the dynamic deployment of many MTD approaches. LSTM predicts the future security incidents of network nodes, which are considered to be the present state of the network. Then, using SMT formalization, we create workable mutated routes and allocated IP address spaces. As a result, activities that are not practicable will be eliminated from the SMDP action space. Next, we work with RM and HAM to develop a new HDRL method for joint mutation. To verify the viability and efficacy of CM-MTD, we lastly carry out a number of simulations and put the proof-of-concept prototype system into use.

We will look into ways to increase attack prediction accuracy in our upcoming work. Furthermore, we will talk about the incentive design to accelerate up CM-MTD's convergence in particular and enable our approach to swiftly adjust to new environments.

References

1. Philip, N.Y., Rodrigues, J.J.P.C., Wang, H., Fong, S.J., Chen, J.: Internet of things for in-home health monitoring systems: current advances, challenges and future directions. IEEE J. Sel. Areas Commun. **39**(2), 300–310 (2021)
2. Mihai, S., Yaqoob, M., Hung, D.V., Davis, W., Towakel, P., Raza, M., Karamanoglu, M., Barn, B., Shetve, D., Prasad, R.V., et al.: Digital twins: a survey on enabling technologies, challenges, trends and future prospects. IEEE Commun. Surv. Tutor. **24**(4), 2255–2291 (2022)
3. Wu, Y., Zhang, K., Zhang, Y.: Digital twin networks: a survey. IEEE Internet Things J. **8**(18), 13789–13804 (2021)
4. Khan, L.U., Han, Z., Saad, W., Hossain, E., Guizani, M., Hong, C.S.: Digital twin of wireless systems: overview, taxonomy, challenges, and opportunities. IEEE Commun. Surv. Tutor. **24**(4), 2230–2254 (2022)
5. Alcaraz, C., Lopez, J.: Digital twin: a comprehensive survey of security threats. IEEE Commun. Surv. Tutor. **24**(3), 1475–1503 (2022)

References

6. Almeaibed, S., Al-Rubaye, S., Tsourdos, A., Avdelidis, N.P.: Digital twin analysis to promote safety and security in autonomous vehicles. IEEE Commun. Stand. Mag. **5**(1), 40–46 (2021)
7. Cho, J.-H., Sharma, D.P., Alavizadeh, H., Yoon, S., Ben-Asher, N., Moore, T.J., Kim, D.S., Lim, H., Nelson, F.F.: Toward proactive, adaptive defense: a survey on moving target defense. IEEE Commun. Surv. Tutor. **22**(1), 709–745 (2020)
8. Zhang, T., Xu, C., Zou, P., Tian, H., Kuang, X., Yang, S., Zhong, L., Niyato, D.: How to mitigate ddos intelligently in sd-iov: a moving target defense approach. IEEE Trans. Indust. Inform. **19**(1), 1097–1106 (2022)
9. Zhang, T., Xu, C., Zhang, B., Shen, J., Kuang, X., Grieco, L.A.: Toward attack-resistant route mutation for vanets: an online and adaptive multiagent reinforcement learning approach. IEEE Trans. Intell. Transp. Syst. **23**(12), 23254–23267 (2022)
10. Xu, C., Zhang, T., Kuang, X., Zhou, Z., Yu, S.: Context-aware adaptive route mutation scheme: a reinforcement learning approach. IEEE Internet Things J. **8**(17), 13528–13541 (2021)
11. Cvitić, I., Perakovic, D., Gupta, B.B., Choo, K.-K.R.: Boosting-based ddos detection in internet of things systems. IEEE Internet Things J. **9**(3), 2109–2123 (2021)
12. Sharma, D.P., Kim, D.S., Yoon, S., Lim, H., Cho, J.-H., Moore, T.J.: Frvm: flexible random virtual ip multiplexing in software-defined networks. In: 2018 17th IEEE International Conference on Trust, Security and Privacy in Computing and Communications/12th IEEE International Conference on Big Data Science and Engineering (TrustCom/BigDataSE), pp. 579–587. IEEE (2018)
13. Dishington, C., Sharma, D.P., Kim, D.S., Cho, J.-H., Moore, T.J., Nelson, F.F.: Security and performance assessment of ip multiplexing moving target defence in software defined networks. In: 2019 18th IEEE International Conference on Trust, Security and Privacy in Computing and Communications/13th IEEE International Conference on Big Data Science and Engineering (TrustCom/BigDataSE), pp. 288–295. IEEE (2019)
14. Wang, H., Li, F., Chen, S.: Towards cost-effective moving target defense against ddos and covert channel attacks. In: Proceedings of the 2016 ACM Workshop on Moving Target Defense, pp. 15–25 (2016)
15. Zhang, T., Xu, v, Zhang, B., Kuang, X., Wang, Y., Yang, S., Muntean, G.-M.: Dq-rm: deep reinforcement learning-based route mutation scheme for multimedia services. In: 2020 International Wireless Communications and Mobile Computing (IWCMC), pp. 291–296. IEEE (2020)
16. Wu, S., Wang, B., Wang, Z., Fan, S., Yang, J., Li, J.: Joint prediction on security event and time interval through deep learning. Comput. Secur. **117**, 102696 (2022)
17. Yi, L., Yin, M., Darbandi, M.: A deep and systematic review of the intrusion detection systems in the fog environment. Trans. Emerg. Telecommun. Technol. **34**(1), e4632 (2023)
18. Kingma, D.P.: Adam: a method for stochastic optimization (2014). arXiv preprint arXiv:1412.6980
19. Schulman, J., Wolski, F., Dhariwal, P., Radford, A., Klimov, O.: Proximal policy optimization algorithms (2017). arXiv preprint arXiv:1707.06347
20. Mnih, V., Kavukcuoglu, K., Silver, D., Rusu, A.A., Veness, J., Bellemare, M.G., Graves, A., Riedmiller, M., Fidjeland, A.K., Ostrovski, G., et al.: Human-level control through deep reinforcement learning. Nature **518**(7540), 529–533 (2015)
21. Fontes, R.R., Afzal, S., Brito, S.H.B., Santos, M.A.S., Rothenberg, C.E.: Mininet-wifi: emulating software-defined wireless networks. In: 2015 11th International Conference on Network and Service Management (CNSM), pp. 384–389. IEEE (2015)
22. Ryu: Ryu sdn framework. https://ryu-sdn.org/. Accessed 20 April 2022
23. Hagberg, A., Swart, P.J., Schult, D.A.: Exploring network structure, dynamics, and function using networkx. Technical report, Los Alamos National Laboratory (LANL), Los Alamos (2008)
24. Zhang, T., Xu, C., Zhang, B., Li, X., Kuang, X., Grieco, L.A.: Towards attack-resistant service function chain migration: a model-based adaptive proximal policy optimization approach. IEEE Trans. Dependable Secure Comput. **20**(6), 4913–4927 (2023)

25. Luo, Q., Luan, T.H., Shi, W., Fan, P.: Deep reinforcement learning based computation offloading and trajectory planning for multi-uav cooperative target search. IEEE J. Sel. Areas Commun. **41**(2), 504–520 (2022)
26. Sharafaldin, I., Lashkari, A.H., Ghorbani, A.A., et al.: Toward generating a new intrusion detection dataset and intrusion traffic characterization. ICISSp **1**, 108–116 (2018)
27. Wu, J., Deng, H.-Z., Tan, Y.-J., Zhu, D.-Z.: Vulnerability of complex networks under intentional attack with incomplete information. J. Phys. A: Math. Theor. **40**(11), 2665 (2007)
28. Kang, M.S., Lee, S.B., Gligor, V.D.: The crossfire attack. In: 2013 IEEE Symposium on Security and Privacy, pp. 127–141. IEEE (2013)
29. iPerf: iperf: the tcp, udp and sctp network bandwidth measurement tool. https://iperf.fr/. Accessed 20 April 2022

Chapter 4
AI-Driven Moving Target Defense Framework for SD-IoV: Roadside Unit Mutation via Proximal Policy Optimization

Abstract Driven by AI, the concept of MTD has gained attention as an effective means to strengthen the protection of complex and dynamically evolving cyber-physical infrastructures. One notable application scenario is the SD-IoV, a critical enabler of the broader IIoT. Traditional security strategies often operate reactively—only responding after intrusions—which weakens their capability against adaptive and sophisticated cyber threats. To overcome these limitations, this work presents a novel AI-enhanced MTD architecture that adaptively reconfigures network states to obscure system exposure and reduce vulnerability in SD-IoV settings. Compared with existing MTD methods that lack flexibility and exhibit low autonomy, our design leverages DRL to autonomously explore and select optimal reconfiguration policies, moving beyond fixed defense-response schemas. In our design, the operation logic of RSUs is abstracted as a MDP, which empowers them to make context-aware decisions in fluctuating environments. Moreover, we incorporate a vehicle-level trust assessment component, which helps detect and isolate suspicious participants—such as compromised or surveillance vehicles—post adaptation. Simulation-based validation reveals that the proposed AI-oriented MTD mechanism significantly outperforms standard approaches in countering DDoS attacks, showcasing its practical advantage in proactive defense.

Keywords Moving target defense · Software defined Internet of vehicles · Deep reinforcement learning · Trust assessment · Distributed denial-of-service

4.1 Introduction

4.1.1 Motivations

With the rapid advancement of VANETs, the Internet of Vehicles (IoV) has emerged as a novel paradigm that has drawn increasing attention in recent years [1]. Serving as a pivotal component of the IIoT, IoV connects vehicles to diverse sensing modules and communication interfaces [2], thereby facilitating dense and concurrent interactions among automobiles and roadside entities. These interactions are typically classified into Vehicle-to-Vehicle (V2V) and Vehicle-to-Infrastructure (V2I) communications, jointly establishing a highly integrated vehicular communication network. To efficiently handle the complexities inherent in such dynamic vehicular systems, there is a pressing need for flexible and intelligent management mechanisms. In this regard, SDN has been recognized as an effective approach, as it decouples the control layer from data transmission processes and offers centralized orchestration and programmability. By merging SDN principles with IoV architecture, the concept of SD-IoV has been introduced, inheriting the architectural benefits of SDN [3]. Within SD-IoV systems, SDN controllers—generally located at base stations—continuously collect real-time data to guide decision-making processes that regulate vehicular communications. Nonetheless, safeguarding both traditional VANETs and emerging SD-IoV infrastructures remains a significant challenge [4]. For instance, DDoS attacks targeting RSUs can critically impair vehicular network stability, which may result in severe misjudgments in data processing. Despite extensive research efforts [5–11] aimed at mitigating DDoS risks in both VANETs and SD-IoV contexts, existing strategies predominantly rely on post-incident responses. Such reactive designs leave systems vulnerable during the reconnaissance phase, where attackers exploit known weaknesses before initiating their assault. Moreover, the growing sophistication of DDoS methods—becoming more stealthy and persistent—further complicates prompt detection and effective defense.

4.1.2 Challenges

To address the previously mentioned security concerns, MTD [12–14] has gained recognition as an effective defensive strategy that persistently reconfigures network settings. In contrast to traditional static defense techniques, MTD introduces unpredictability and system dynamism, which undermines attackers' reliance on prior system knowledge and significantly lowers the probability of successful intrusions. A broad body of research has verified the capability of MTD to strengthen IoT security [15] and to mitigate the impact of DDoS attacks [12, 13, 16]. However, several challenges persist in current MTD methodologies. First, many existing MTD solutions fail to adapt to highly dynamic environments. For instance, MTD applications for IoT often assume a stable network topology, while those targeting DDoS attacks are primarily designed for static web applications. The inherently dynamic nature of SD-IoV's wireless environment poses a substantial obstacle to conventional MTD approaches. Second, most current MTD strategies lack the sophistication needed for real-time decision-making, as they heavily depend on predefined models of attack-defense scenarios. Furthermore, existing solutions face difficulties in quickly tracing the origins of DDoS attacks and in accurately identifying malicious entities, such as rogue vehicles. This reveals the need for a more

4.1 Introduction

intelligent security management system that integrates the dynamic characteristics of mobile networks like SD-IoV with cutting-edge AI-based defense techniques. This evolution presents an opportunity for deeper research into how AI can enhance MTD in such contexts [17].

4.1.3 Contributions

This paper presents an MTD mechanism empowered by artificial intelligence to defend against DDoS threats in SD-IoV networks. The distinguishing feature of our design lies in its adaptive modification of RSU-side network configurations, guided by DRL, coupled with a recurrent evaluation of vehicle trustworthiness following RSU-to-vehicle reallocation. Recent progress in DRL has shown strong capability in addressing decision-making challenges under dynamic vehicular conditions [18]. Leveraging this, the proposed intelligent MTD framework suppresses DDoS impacts on authorized vehicles while simultaneously detecting and segregating malicious entities. By tackling DDoS risks at their origin, this approach enhances overall network resilience. To the best of our knowledge, this is the first MTD solution that intelligently adapts to the heterogeneous and ever-changing landscape of SD-IoV. In summary, the primary contributions of this study are as follows:

1. We design a flexible configuration adaptation mechanism, where the adjustment of RSU-related parameters, such as communication ranges and capacity limits—is formulated as a MDP. The process of refining these configurations is modeled as an optimization objective. Relying on this structure, we employ DRL to identify the most efficient configuration adjustment strategy.
2. To effectively differentiate between malicious and legitimate vehicles, we propose a periodic trust evaluation approach that re-assesses RSU-vehicle associations after each dynamic reshuffle. Considering the rapidly changing characteristics of SD-IoV, we define a set of network constraints for the reshuffling process using SMT [19], including criteria such as link reachability, node accessibility, unpredictability, and capacity bounds.
3. To examine the effectiveness of our intelligent MTD framework, we conduct extensive experiments through the NS-3 network simulator. The simulation outcomes confirm that the proposed strategy performs better than existing approaches and shows strong adaptability to SD-IoV scenarios.

4.1.4 Related Work

In both conventional VANETs and the more advanced SD-IoV scenarios, maintaining the security of vehicular networks remains a critical issue requiring immediate and sustained attention. Numerous countermeasures have been proposed to tackle these pressing security threats. For example, Mejri et al. [5] developed a detection technique for greedy behavior in highly dynamic network settings through a two-phase strategy—one focused on suspicion assessment and the other on decision inference using fuzzy logic and linear regression. However, these methods were primarily tailored for VANETs and may lack adaptability in the highly dynamic conditions of SD-IoV environments. In SD-IoV settings, Biasi et al. [6] adopted a time-series analysis strategy to trace spoofed packet origins and reduce DDoS impacts. Other researchers have explored trust-based mechanisms to enhance vehicular network resilience [7]. For instance, Xia et al. [8] introduced a trust inference approach that combines subjective feedback with recommendation systems to evaluate vehicle credibility. In a similar vein, Nigam et al. [9] proposed an AI-enhanced routing protocol based on trust, employing multi-objective optimization to guard against threats from abnormal nodes. Despite these contributions, most existing defenses follow a reactive paradigm, where countermeasures are triggered only after attacks have taken place. This delay provides adversaries with ample time to analyze system vulnerabilities and launch effective attacks, thereby weakening the overall robustness of the defense mechanisms.

Fortunately, MTD has become an increasingly adopted and effective approach. Its fundamental idea lies in dynamically modifying network components or structural configurations, thereby introducing randomness and unpredictability that hinder adversaries from executing reliable attack strategies. Within the IoT landscape, Duan et al. [15] proposed a method that randomly adjusts the coverage scope of APs at regular intervals. Beyond addressing general IoT-related security concerns, multiple MTD mechanisms have also been crafted to combat targeted threats such as DDoS attacks. For instance, Zhou et al. [16] advocated for dynamic management of device access permissions and migration of service replicas to neutralize DDoS threats close to their source. In another line of work, Zhang et al. [12–14] proposed a smart routing mutation method that enhances mutation decision-making to suppress the impact of DDoS intrusions. Despite these advances, the volatile nature and wireless infrastructure of SD-IoV make it difficult to directly transplant MTD techniques originally crafted for IoT or traditional DDoS defenses.

SD-IoV is now gaining attention as a viable foundation for future IoV-integrated IIoT platforms. While security remains a significant obstacle in SD-IoV systems, MTD offers a fresh perspective for resisting sophisticated network attacks, especially those involving DDoS vectors. Nevertheless, most existing MTD mechanisms lack compatibility with SD-IoV due to their inability to accommodate its dynamic and heterogeneous wireless environment. To bridge this gap, there is a compelling need to devise a customized MTD framework tailored to SD-IoV-specific constraints. To the best of our knowledge, the proposed work constitutes the earliest attempt to design an intelligent MTD solution targeting DDoS mitigation in SD-IoV. Our method further incorporates AI-based trust assessment to effectively distinguish between benign and malicious vehicles.

4.2 Model Formulation on the Edge Layer

In this section, we present the network model and the threat model separately.

4.2.1 Network Model

Figure 4.1 presents the system architecture of SD-IoV, which leverages dynamic reconfiguration to strengthen security. The wireless data plane integrates RSUs and vehicles, both serving as clients within the overall framework. RSUs, embedded with OpenFlow switches, function concurrently as APs that serve the connected vehicles. The control plane is supervised by BSs, where SDN controllers are deployed. Coordination between the control and data planes is realized through the southbound API, enabling timely adjustments to network configurations. In addition to the control and data layers, the system incorporates an application plane responsible for executing services such as security enforcement, Internet access, and other application logic within the data center. The northbound API decomposes network operations into fine-grained controller tasks, offering flexibility to manage

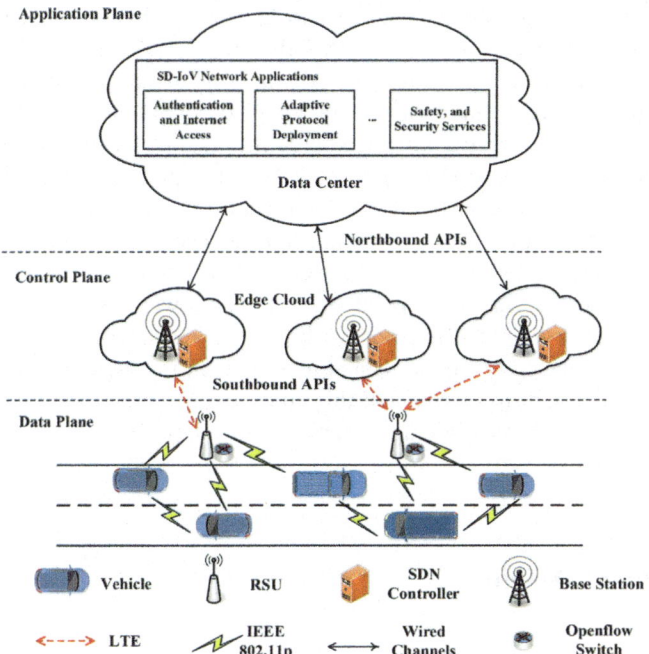

Fig. 4.1 The structural design of SD-IoV

dynamic network updates. This architecture enables AI-based intelligent decision-making that promotes both security reinforcement and operational efficiency.

We study an SD-IoV scenario composed of n RSUs, m vehicles, and k BSs. The SD-IoV topology is represented by an undirected graph $\mathbb{G} = (\mathcal{N}, \mathcal{M}, \mathcal{K}, \mathcal{E})$, where: (1) $\mathcal{N}$ stands for the RSU node set n_i, with $1 \leq i \leq n$; (2) $\mathcal{M}$ indicates the collection of vehicle nodes v_j, where $1 \leq j \leq m$; (3) $\mathcal{K}$ corresponds to the BS node set b_x, with $1 \leq x \leq k$; (4) $\mathcal{E}$ describes the wireless link set e that interconnects different node types. In this setting, vehicles move according to the Manhattan mobility model [20]. Nevertheless, our method remains effective under alternative mobility assumptions, as its design does not depend on any fixed movement pattern. Both BSs and RSUs are evenly placed throughout the selected simulation area.

4.2.2 Threat Model

This study explores a complex attack model under the SD-IoV framework, where the adversary adopts two distinct malicious roles. The first role corresponds to a spy vehicle that connects with RSUs and quietly collects critical data—such as IP addresses and geographic coordinates—while avoiding any overtly malicious behavior. The second role operates as an active infrastructure that exploits the intelligence obtained by the spy vehicles to launch bandwidth-intensive or volumetric DDoS attacks targeting designated RSUs. As a result, all vehicles associated with the compromised RSUs suffer from disruptions in service connectivity. This combined tactic is referred to as a spy-enabled DDoS attack. The adversary can deploy several aggressive infrastructures throughout the impacted area, each exhibiting greater transmission strength than the participating vehicles and RSUs in the network. Vehicles are converted into spying entities either by voluntarily joining the attacker's ecosystem or by being compromised. These spy vehicles periodically relay gathered intelligence to the attacker-controlled infrastructures. RSUs remain particularly vulnerable in this context due to their lower resilience compared to high-cost BSs, as highlighted in prior work [15]. A visual example of such DDoS attacks, jointly executed by spy units and malicious infrastructures, is illustrated in Fig. 4.2. It is important to clarify that this study does not delve into control plane vulnerabilities, as they have already been comprehensively addressed in previous literature [21–23].

4.3 Detailed Design

To effectively mitigate spy-enabled DDoS attacks, we design a smart MTD framework. Unlike existing defense strategies in SD-IoV [6], our approach not only alleviates the impact of DDoS attacks but also introduces a trust evaluation module to identify potential spy vehicles. The internal structure of the proposed MTD

4.3 Detailed Design

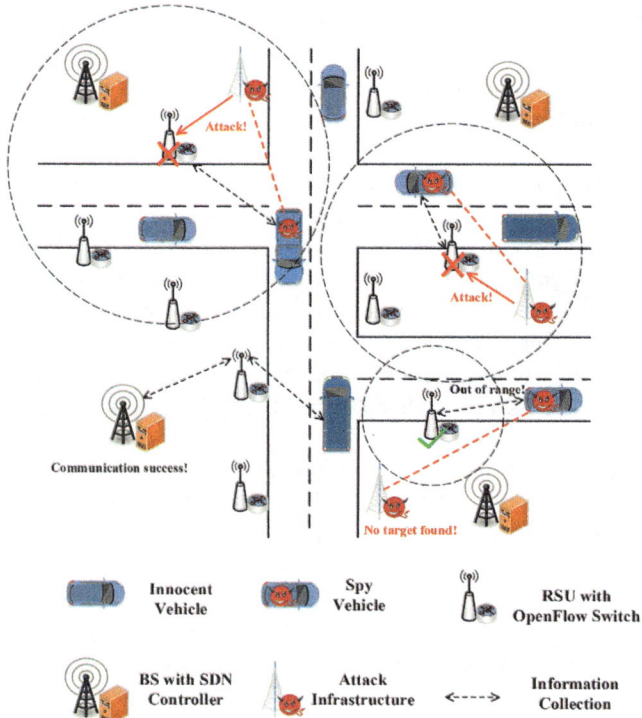

Fig. 4.2 An example of attack scenario

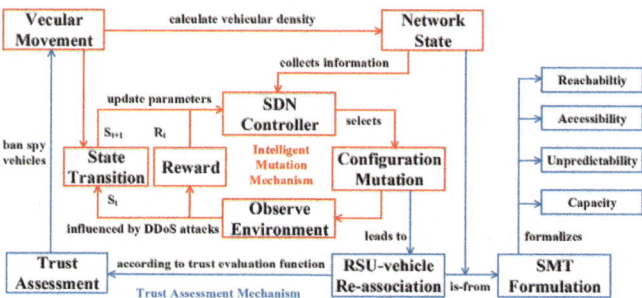

Fig. 4.3 Framework of our proposed MTD scheme

framework is depicted in Fig. 4.3. In this figure, the red portion illustrates the operational flow of the adaptive mutation logic, while the blue portion represents the execution of the vehicle trust verification module. The mutation logic component dynamically tunes RSU network settings through DRL. Meanwhile, the trust evaluation module assesses the reliability of vehicles after RSU-to-vehicle reassignment. Further details regarding these two modules are elaborated in Sects. 4.3.1 and 4.3.2.

4.3.1 Intelligent Mutation Mechanism

The objective of this mechanism is to improve RSU configuration deployment through DRL, with the intent of minimizing the number of vehicles impacted by DDoS attacks. As shown in Fig. 4.3, the SDN controller gathers information related to vehicular traffic load, which reflects the current condition of the network. Using this information, the controller selects updated RSU settings, tracks the evolution of system states, and receives feedback in the form of rewards. These rewards are then used to adjust the parameters of the underlying neural network. After running for a sufficient number of learning steps, the SDN controller converges to a set of optimized RSU settings. We define this adaptive mutation strategy as the **P**roximal **P**olicy **O**ptimization algorithm for **O**ptimal **C**onfiguration **M**utation (PPO-OCM). Below, we shall discuss the further technical details of this approach in greater depth.

We begin by formulating the configuration mutation as a MDP. Then, the objective of discovering the optimal RSU configuration is reframed as an optimization task. Finally, we introduce the PPO-OCM algorithm, which is designed to handle this optimization.

We divide time into discrete, equal-length intervals of duration ΔT, with each step indexed by $t \in \{0, 1, 2, \dots\}$. In this part, we describe how vehicular mobility induces configuration updates and represent it as an MDP to reflect the system's dynamic behavior. The key elements of this MDP framework are described below:

State Space The physical region under consideration is partitioned into square units of equal size, referred to as grids. Each grid captures a distinct level of vehicular presence. Suppose the total number of grids is h. The state at time t is described by the vehicular density vector $S_t = \{s_1, s_2, \dots, s_h\}$, where s_z ($1 \leq z \leq h$) denotes the vehicle count within grid z. Given that the area contains m vehicles overall, the dimensionality of the state space is given by the binomial coefficient $\binom{m+h-1}{h-1}$, which increases with the total vehicle population. To handle the resulting scalability challenge, we adopt DRL, as elaborated in Sect. 4.2.2.

Action Space The RSU network settings, including communication radii and access limits, are periodically updated over time. An action refers to selecting a global configuration for all RSUs, denoted by $\mathcal{A}_t = [\tilde{R}_t^{rsu}, \tilde{Q}_t^{rsu}]$, where $\tilde{R}_t^{rsu} = \{R_{t,1}^{rsu}, R_{t,2}^{rsu}, \dots, R_{t,n}^{rsu}\}$ defines the communication ranges, and $\tilde{Q}_t^{rsu} = \{Q_{t,1}^{rsu}, Q_{t,2}^{rsu}, \dots, Q_{t,n}^{rsu}\}$ specifies the access quotas (i.e., the upper bound on the number of vehicles that can associate with each RSU). The communication radii are selected from the set $\alpha_1, \dots, \alpha_k$, while access quotas are chosen from $\beta_1, \dots, \beta_l$, all of which are natural numbers. Enlarging both the communication range and access quota permits more vehicles to connect to an RSU, though this also incurs greater energy cost. In the event of a successful DDoS attack, such configurations expose more vehicles to risk. Conversely, reducing these parameters yields fewer connections and lower exposure. The overall size of the action space is $k^n l^n$, which

4.3 Detailed Design

increases exponentially with the RSU count. Solutions to handle this scalability challenge are discussed in Sect. 4.2.2.

State Transitions As vehicles traverse the region, they pass through a sequence of spatial grids. The transition of a vehicle from one grid cell to another within each time slot is regarded as a state update.

Reward Function At each time step t, when a new RSU configuration is applied, the total reward $\mathcal{R}_t$ is computed by integrating three components: service quality, energy usage, and system security. The reward function is defined as: $\mathcal{R}_t = \alpha \mathcal{R}_t^n - \beta \mathcal{R}_t^e - \zeta \mathcal{R}_t^s$, where α, β, and ζ are weighting parameters. The first term $\mathcal{R}_t^n$ reflects service capacity and is computed as $\sum_{i \in \mathcal{N}} \mathbb{N}_{t,i}$, where $\mathbb{N}_{t,i}$ denotes the number of vehicles associated with RSU n_i at time t, constrained by the limit $\mathbb{N}_{t,i} \leq Q_{t,i}^{rsu}$. The second component $\mathcal{R}_t^e$ evaluates energy cost and is defined as $\sum_{i \in \mathcal{N}} \mathbb{E}(R_{t,i})$, where $\mathbb{E}(R_{t,i})$ characterizes the energy consumed for communication at RSU i with range $R_{t,i}$. Following [24], $\mathbb{E}(R_{t,i})$ is formulated as:

$$\mathbb{E}(R_{t,i}) = \begin{cases} \sum_{\mathbb{N}_{t,i}} \Phi_t \cdot (E_{elec} + \epsilon_f R_{t,i}^2), & R_{t,i} \leq R_d \\ \sum_{\mathbb{N}_{t,i}} \Phi_t \cdot (E_{elec} + \epsilon_t R_{t,i}^4), & R_{t,i} > R_d \end{cases}$$

Here, Φ_t indicates the volume of data sent from RSU i to each linked vehicle at time t, and $E_{elec}, \epsilon_f, \epsilon_t$ are system-defined constants. R_d is a threshold range, typically set to 75 m. The final term $\mathcal{R}_t^s$ measures the degradation in service due to adversarial attacks and is defined as $\sum_{i \in \mathcal{N}} Y_{t,i} \cdot \mathbb{N}_{t,i}$, where $Y_{t,i}$ is a binary indicator: it takes value 1 if RSU n_i is compromised at time t, and 0 otherwise.

The goal of performing configuration mutation is to determine the best RSU setting that yields the highest cumulative reward from the surrounding environment. Based on this formulation, the corresponding optimization problem is given below:

$$\mathbf{P1}: \max_{\pi} \mathbf{E}_{\pi} \left[\sum_{k=0}^{\infty} \gamma^k \mathcal{R}_{t+k} \right], \quad (4.1)$$

where π denotes the decision-making policy responsible for choosing actions under different mutated configurations, $\mathbf{E}$ is the expectation operator, and γ represents the discount coefficient ranging from 0 to 1.

Theoretically, the optimization problem P1 could be tackled using approaches such as dynamic programming or exhaustive search. However, due to the dynamic nature of vehicle movements, it becomes impractical to directly track the state transition probabilities required for the computation. In recent years, RL has demonstrated significant potential in deriving optimal policies for MDPs, making it a suitable candidate for solving such optimization challenges. In the following section, we explore the rationale behind utilizing RL within the context of SD-IoV. Given that vehicles are predominantly human-driven, they tend to frequent specific locations, such as residential areas, workplaces, etc. This behavior reveals that vehicle mobility follows a pattern of temporal locality, which mirrors the mobility trends of humans [25]. Building upon the findings in [26], it has been noted that the vehicle density within each grid tends to remain stable across different days. As a result, the historical movement patterns of vehicles exhibit a high degree of regularity. Additionally, the movement behavior of spy vehicles often mirrors that of non-suspicious vehicles, since their main goal is to blend in and evade detection. Consequently, during the RL training phase, the environment will not adversely affect the convergence process, as the consistency in vehicle movements can be effectively learned. With this in mind, RL can interact with the environment over time to identify the optimal configurations for RSUs, which will later be deployed in practice to enhance the dynamic security of the system.

In this study, we utilize the PPO algorithm to address the optimization task formulated in Problem P1. The detailed pseudo-code implementation of PPO-OCM is presented in **Algorithm 1**. The algorithm starts with an initialization phase, where key elements such as parameter definitions, buffer structures, and DNNs are prepared (lines 1–5). The core execution begins at line 6 and consists of two main stages. The first stage is responsible for collecting experience by interacting with the environment (lines 7–18). Starting from an initial state, the agent evolves over T time steps to form one complete episode (lines 7–8). During this phase, SDN controllers operate under the previous policy $\pi_{\theta_{old}}$ to determine actions that modify RSU configurations. Corresponding rewards are recorded (lines 9–12), and transitions are logged into the buffer. Subsequently, the advantage and value estimates are computed using the generalized advantage estimation technique (lines 13–16). The second stage deals with training the policy based on the stored experience. Gradients of both the policy and value networks are calculated separately and used to refine the associated model parameters (lines 19–24). Finally, a policy update step is performed at line 25.

4.3.2 Trust Assessment Mechanism

This mechanism aims to detect the presence of spy vehicles through trust evaluation conducted after the RSU-vehicle binding relationships have been randomized. Notably, due to behavioral differences, spy vehicles are more likely to attempt connections with compromised RSUs compared to benign ones. As the system evolves, this tendency causes a divergence in the observed trust metrics between normal and malicious vehicles, serving as a distinguishing indicator. Following each configuration update, vehicles are reassigned to RSUs while adhering to a set of predefined constraints. This reassignment process is cast as a constraint satisfaction problem and solved using SMT. Specifically, the Z3 solver is employed to derive valid RSU-vehicle association schemes [27]. After the new pairings are established, trust scores are re-evaluated for each vehicle. Eventually, vehicles identified as suspicious are prevented from reconnecting to RSUs. The complete procedure is

4.3 Detailed Design

Algorithm 3 PPO-OCM

1: Set parameters ξ, ϵ, and γ.
2: Set batch size T and minibatch size K.
3: Initialize the experience replay buffer $\mathcal{B} = \varnothing$.
4: Randomly initialize Critic network $V(\mathcal{S}, \phi)$.
5: Randomly initialize Actor network π_θ with weight θ.
6: **for** $iteration = 1, 2, \cdots$ **do**
7:    **for** $episode = 1, 2, \cdots, K$ **do**
8:       **for** $t = 0, 1, \cdots, T-1$ **do**
9:          Obtain the current network state $\mathcal{S}_t$.
10:         Run policy $\pi_{\theta_{old}}$ to select action $\mathcal{A}_t$.
11:         Execute the configuration mutation for RSUs.
12:         Observe the outcome reward $\mathcal{R}_t$.
13:         Obtain the next network state $\mathcal{S}_{t+1}$.
14:         Collect $\mathcal{U}_t = (\mathcal{S}_t, \mathcal{A}_t, \mathcal{R}_t, \mathcal{S}_{t+1})$, and $\mathcal{B} \cup \mathcal{U}_t$.
15:         Calculate δ_t and $\hat{A}_t = \sum_{q \geq t}^{K} (\gamma\xi)^{q-t}\delta_q$.
16:         Estimate $\hat{V}_t = \hat{A}_i + V(\mathcal{S}_t, \phi)$.
17:       **end for**
18:    **end for**
19:    **for** $epoch = 1, 2, \cdots, U$ **do**
20:       Compute the actor loss:

$$\mathcal{J}_a = \frac{1}{T} \sum_{i=1}^{T} \min(r_i, \text{clip}(r_i, 1-\epsilon, 1+\epsilon)) \hat{A}_i.$$

21:       Update θ by $\nabla_\theta \mathcal{J}_a$.
22:       Compute the critic loss:

$$\mathcal{J}_c = -\frac{1}{T} \sum_{i=1}^{T} (\hat{V}_i - V(\mathcal{S}_i, \phi))^2.$$

23:       Update ϕ by $\nabla_\phi \mathcal{J}_c$.
24:    **end for**
25:    Update $\pi_{\theta_{old}} \leftarrow \pi_\theta$.
26: **end for**

formalized as the **T**rust **A**ssessment algorithm for **R**SU-**V**ehicle **A**ssociations (TA-RVA), with further technical elaboration available below.

PPO-OCM mitigates the effects of DDoS threats by adaptively reconfiguring RSU parameters, thereby triggering new associations between vehicles and RSUs. This adaptive strategy facilitates the identification of malicious and legitimate vehicles during the credibility evaluation phase of each reassignment cycle, effectively curbing DDoS attempts at an early stage. In this section, we present the method for reallocating RSU-vehicle links and assessing vehicle reliability throughout the reassignment routine. Given the ever-changing nature of SD-IoV wireless conditions, we first formulate a set of network constraints using SMT. Subsequently, a tailored trust evaluation mechanism is introduced to accommodate these restrictions.

In this subsection, we formulate the reorganization of RSU-vehicle associations as a constraint satisfaction problem. Let the boolean variable $f_{t,j}^i$ indicate whether vehicle v_j is associated with RSU n_i at time slot t. If the connection exists, then $f_{t,j}^i$ is set to 1; otherwise, it is assigned 0. Considering realistic network factors, the reassignment of RSU-vehicle links must adhere to a set of formalized constraints, which are expressed using SMT.

Reachability Constraint: Vehicles are capable of establishing connections to RSUs within an N-hop communication range. Two typical scenarios describe the connection behavior: (1) If a vehicle is located within the service range of an RSU, it forms a direct link; (2) If the vehicle lies outside the coverage of all RSUs, it relies on nearby vehicles to relay the connection request until a valid link is formed.

Therefore, the reachability constraint can be expressed as:

$$f_{t,j}^i \cdot \mathcal{D}(n_i, v_j) \leq \mathcal{W}_{t,i}, \forall n_i \in \mathcal{N}, \forall v_j \in \mathcal{M}, \tag{4.2}$$

where $\mathcal{D}(n_i, v_j)$ indicates the physical distance between RSU n_i and vehicle v_j. The symbol $\mathcal{W}_{t,i}$ denotes the upper bound of the communication range for RSU n_i, defined as:

$$\mathcal{W}_{t,i} = \begin{cases} \sum_{j \in N-1} R_{t,j}^v + R_{t,i}^{rsu}, & R_{t,i}^{rsu} \leq R_{t,j}^v, \\ \sum_{j \in N} R_{t,j}^v, & R_{t,i}^{rsu} > R_{t,j}^v, \end{cases} \tag{4.3}$$

Here, $R_{t,i}^{rsu}$ denotes the communication capability of RSU n_i at time t, as produced by PPO-OCM. The term $R_{t,j}^v$ refers to the range of vehicle v_j at the same time slot, and N represents the allowed maximum number of hops.

Accessibility Constraint Each vehicle must form a connection with an RSU, and the corresponding condition is expressed as:

$$\sum_{n_i \in \mathcal{N}} \sum_{v_j \in \mathcal{M}} f_{t,j}^i = m, \sum_{n_i \in \mathcal{N}} f_{t,j}^i = 1, \forall v_j \in \mathcal{M}, \tag{4.4}$$

where m denotes the total number of vehicles. The first expression ensures that all vehicles are successfully assigned to RSUs after the association reconfiguration. The second expression restricts each vehicle to connect with exactly one RSU in each time frame.

To enhance unpredictability, the model reduces the association similarity between adjacent time slots, and the formulation is given below:

$$\mathbb{D}_{n \times m}^{t,t+1} \triangleq \begin{bmatrix} d_{1,1}^{t,t+1} & \cdots & d_{1,m}^{t,t+1} \\ \vdots & \ddots & \vdots \\ d_{n,1}^{t,t+1} & \cdots & d_{n,m}^{t,t+1} \end{bmatrix}, \tag{4.5}$$

4.3 Detailed Design

$$\sum_{n_i \in \mathcal{N}} \sum_{v_j \in \mathcal{M}} (d_{i,j}^{t,t+1})^2 \geq \Psi, \tag{4.6}$$

Here, $\mathbb{D}_{n \times m}^{t,t+1}$ refers to the matrix that quantifies association differences, and $d_{i,j}^{t,t+1} = f_{t+1,j}^i - f_{t,j}^i$ captures the variation in connection decisions across two adjacent time steps. Inequality (4.6) ensures that the aggregate deviation exceeds a predefined threshold Ψ, thereby achieving dynamic association unpredictability.

Capacity Constraint The upper limit on RSU access, denoted by $Q_{t,i}^{rsu}$, is dynamically adjusted according to the PPO-OCM output at time t. The corresponding constraint is formulated as:

$$\sum_{v_j \in \mathcal{M}} f_{t,j}^i \leq Q_{t,i}^{rsu}, \forall n_i \in \mathcal{N}. \tag{4.7}$$

This condition ensures that RSU n_i does not exceed its predefined vehicle-handling capacity, thereby maintaining consistent service performance without overload-induced degradation.

Since the association decision variable $f_{t,j}^i$ is binary and only takes values from {0, 1}, finding a configuration that satisfies all imposed constraints translates into a satisfiability problem, which is proven to be NP-complete [28]. Due to the rapidly changing vehicular topology, SDN controllers must address this problem in a real-time setting. Given the high computational demand of solving NP-complete instances, we utilize the Z3 solver [27] to compute feasible RSU-vehicle assignment results. In general, multiple valid configurations may exist, among which one is selected at random. To distinguish between malicious and benign vehicles, trust metrics are re-evaluated for all vehicles following each reassignment round. Taking into account multiple behavioral indicators, we define the malicious score $\mathcal{T}_{t,j}$ for a specific vehicle v_j at time slot t as:

$$\mathcal{T}_{t,j} = \mu \sum_{\tilde{t}=1}^{t} \sum_{i=1}^{n} f_{\tilde{t},j}^i \mathbf{Y}_{\tilde{t},i} Q_{\tilde{t},i} + \nu \sum_{\tilde{t}=1}^{t} G_{\tilde{t},j} - \xi \sum_{\tilde{t}=1}^{t} \tilde{t}, \tag{4.8}$$

where μ, ν, and ξ are predefined weights. The term $G_{\tilde{t},j}$ denotes the number of DDoS incidents observed by vehicle v_j during time slot $\tilde{t}$. The first component reflects the degree of exposure to compromised RSUs; the higher the RSU capacity, the more severe the impact on the malicious score. The second component accumulates the total DDoS attacks linked to the vehicle, while the third introduces a time-decay factor that reduces the score over time. If the resulting value $\mathcal{T}_{t,j}$ exceeds the threshold Υ, the vehicle v_j is flagged as a spy and is prohibited from initiating any RSU associations.

The detailed procedure of TA-RVA is illustrated in **Algorithm 4**. Initially, the system sets up the malicious score records for all vehicles and determines the

Algorithm 4 TA-RVA: trust-aware RSU-vehicle association mechanism
---
1: Set the initial trust level of every vehicle to zero.
2: Define the feasible matching set as empty.
3: **for** $t = 1$ to T **do**
4:     Select and perform action $\mathcal{A}_t$ following Algorithm 1.
5:     **for** $i = 1$ to n **do**
6:         Obtain $\mathcal{W}_{t,i}$ and $Q^{rsu}_{t,i}$ using PPO-COM framework.
7:     **end for**
8:     Employ the Z3 solver to determine valid RSU-vehicle pairings.
9:     Update RSU IP configurations.
10:     Randomize current RSU-vehicle associations.
11:     **for** $j = 1$ to m **do**
12:         Recalculate the malicious score for vehicle v_j using Equation (4.8).
13:         **if** $\mathcal{T}_{t,j} \geq \Upsilon$ **then**
14:             Classify v_j as a malicious agent and revoke its access.
15:         **end if**
16:     **end for**
17: **end for**

valid RSU-vehicle mappings (lines 1–2). During each time interval, the designated configuration adjustment $\mathcal{A}_t$ is applied (lines 3–4). Then, the values of $\mathcal{W}_{t,i}$ and $Q^{rsu}_{t,i}$ for each RSU are obtained based on the dynamic decisions produced by PPO-OCM (lines 5–7). An SMT-based formulation is established, and the Z3 solver is employed to compute acceptable RSU-vehicle assignment outcomes (line 8). To enhance privacy, the SDN controller reassigns the IP addresses of RSUs [29], thereby obstructing spy vehicles from collecting network identity details (line 9). Subsequently, the controller reconfigures the RSU-to-vehicle bindings (line 10). For every vehicle, its malicious score is re-evaluated using Eq. (4.8). If the score of vehicle v_j surpasses the security threshold Υ, the vehicle is blocked from initiating associations with any RSUs (lines 11–16).

4.4 Performance Evaluation and Analysis

To simulate a realistic urban vehicular environment, a portion of Beijing's city layout is adopted as the scenario background. The chosen region covers an area of $1.8 \times 1.8\,\text{km}^2$, which is segmented into a 3×3 grid to support spatial partitioning. This simulation integrates two mainstream tools: SUMO [30] is used for generating vehicular mobility, while NS-3 [31] is employed to handle network communication. In particular, SUMO generates vehicle trajectories based on a Manhattan-style mobility pattern, which are subsequently imported into NS-3 for conducting network-level analysis. Each simulated vehicle is equipped with two wireless modules—IEEE 802.11p and LTE—to support heterogeneous communication. RSUs are placed every 300 m along the roads, and a BS is deployed at the center of the simulation region. Each grid cell also includes a malicious infrastructure node strategically positioned at its midpoint. The layout of RSUs, the BS, and

4.4 Performance Evaluation and Analysis

Table 4.1 Key settings used in the simulation

Configuration item	Assigned value or range
Simulated region size	1.8×1.8 km^2
Grid cell width	600 m
Duration per slot ΔT, message interval	0.1 s, 0.1 s
Packet size (request/data)	64 byte, 1000 byte
Vehicle speed range	10–60 km/h
Total vehicles m	[50, 60, ..., 100]
Deployed RSUs n	[40, 48]
Number of base stations k	1
Spy nodes deployed	10
Malicious infrastructures	9
Communication range (vehicles, BS)	50 m, 1000 m
RSU transmission range	[50, 60, ..., 100] m
RSU capacity range	[15, 20, 25, 30]
Hop count upper bound N	3
Parameters α, β, ζ	$2, 1 \times 10^{-3}, 0.5$
Parameters $E_{elec}, \epsilon_f, \epsilon_t$	$50, 10, 1.3 \times 10^{-3}$
Trust formula weights μ, ν, ξ	0.4, 1, 1
Malicious score threshold Υ	10,000

Table 4.2 Training settings for PPO-OCM

Setup item	Assigned value
Total training rounds	4000
Steps per round	10
Reward discount γ	0.9
GAE smoothing factor	0.95
Clipping threshold	0.2
Epochs per update	4
Optimizer learning rate (Adam)	0.005
Actor network layer size	[256]
Critic network layer size	[16]
Activation used	$tanh$
Output activation	$softmax$

adversarial nodes is rendered using NetAnim 3.108 [32]. The BS additionally hosts the SDN controller, which is responsible for executing the PPO-OCM and TA-RVA schemes. In each simulation cycle, the controller selects a modified configuration and computes optimized RSU-vehicle assignments, dispatching control messages to all RSUs under its scope. Once instructed, RSUs update their configurations and reconnect with assigned vehicles. To facilitate deep reinforcement learning in NS-3, the NS3gym framework [33] is integrated, enabling tight linkage with OpenAI Gym. Table 4.1 summarizes the main SD-IoV configuration settings, while Table 4.2 presents key neural network hyperparameters.

It is worth noting that, to the best of our knowledge, no existing MTD approaches have been specifically designed for direct application in SD-IoV environments. Consequently, we choose a set of representative baseline methods that, although not originally intended for SD-IoV, can be adapted to this context for comparative evaluation:

- **RNM** [15]: This baseline employs a network agility strategy in which the transmission range of RSUs is dynamically and randomly varied. By intermittently altering RSU coverage areas, vehicles are compelled to reassociate with different RSUs over time. The primary objective is to introduce uncertainty for potential attackers by making RSU availability appear unpredictable and transient.
- **TIM** [8]: This method adopts a trust assessment mechanism built upon an inference framework that combines both direct (subjective) trust and indirect (recommendation-based) trust information to evaluate the reliability of network entities.
- **CACA** [34]: This scheme focuses on optimizing handoff decisions with the objective of maximizing the minimum achievable throughput among all mobile nodes, thereby enhancing fairness in network resource allocation.

4.4.1 Defense Performance

Attack Strength serves as a key indicator for assessing the effectiveness of defense mechanisms. It is quantified as the total capacity of RSUs that are successfully compromised by adversaries. To evaluate and compare performance, we simulate 2000 independent episodes, computing the Attack Strength in each case under three different defense strategies: PPO-OCM, RNM, and TIM.

As illustrated in Fig. 4.4, the Attack Strength under the TIM strategy remains virtually unchanged throughout all episodes, maintaining a steady level near 250. This consistency arises from the static nature of TIM, where RSUs operate with fixed coverage ranges and capacity settings, resulting in an unvarying Attack Strength. In the case of RNM, Attack Strength exhibits significant fluctuations across episodes, averaging around 225. This variability stems from RNM's periodic adjustments to RSU transmission ranges and access capacities, which moderately mitigate Attack Strength levels. Conversely, the PPO-OCM approach demonstrates a noticeable downward trend in Attack Strength, dropping from approximately 235 to 200 as training progresses. This reduction reflects the ability of deep reinforcement learning to iteratively discover more effective RSU configurations that suppress attack impact. Convergence is observed after roughly 1000 simulation episodes. These experimental findings clearly indicate that PPO-OCM achieves superior performance compared to both RNM and TIM in minimizing the attack strength of DDoS threats.

4.4 Performance Evaluation and Analysis

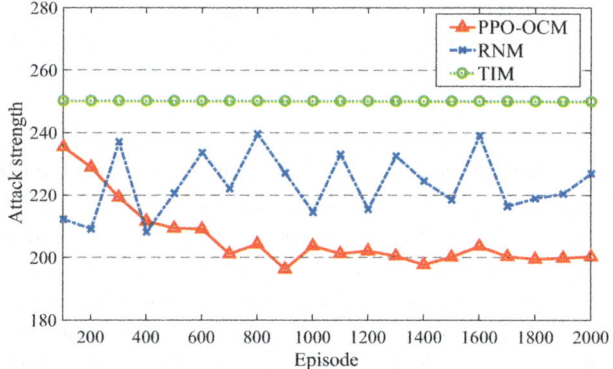

Fig. 4.4 Defense performance comparison

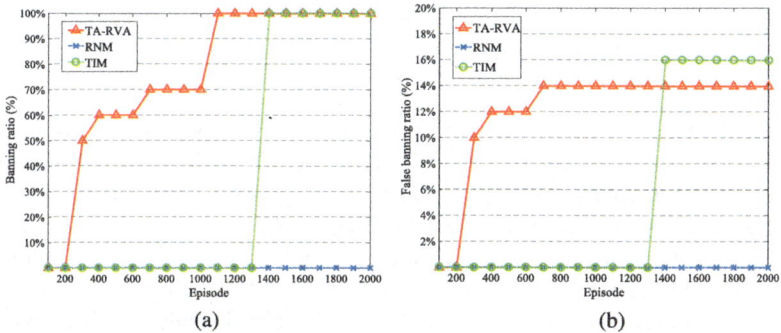

Fig. 4.5 Trustworthiness performance comparison. (**a**) Banning ratio. (**b**) False banning ratio

4.4.2 Trustworthiness Performance

The effectiveness of the proposed TA-RVA strategy lies in its capability to accurately detect and block spy vehicles while ensuring that authorized users retain access. This performance is assessed based on the precision of the trust-based decision module, as described in [35]. To evaluate this aspect, two metrics are introduced: the banning ratio (BR) and the false banning ratio (FBR). BR indicates the percentage of malicious vehicles that are correctly removed from the network, relative to the total number of adversarial participants. Conversely, FBR reflects the share of legitimate vehicles mistakenly excluded from the overall pool of normal users. A total of 2000 simulation runs are conducted, during which both BR and FBR statistics are collected across three comparative schemes: TA-RVA, RNM, and TIM. It is worth emphasizing that RNM does not include any trust inference module; as a result, its BR and FBR scores remain zero throughout all evaluations.

As shown in Fig. 4.5a, TA-RVA's BR steadily increases during the simulation and ultimately reaches 100% after about 1100 episodes. This trend is driven by the consistent behavior of spy vehicles, which frequently exploit adversarial infrastructures to launch DDoS attacks—accelerating the growth of their malicious scores. In comparison, TIM requires roughly 1300 episodes to reach the same BR level, reflecting a slower identification process for malicious participants. TA-RVA achieves earlier and more efficient elimination of threats by requiring fewer episodes to complete the banning process. Figure 4.5b further shows that the FBR under TA-RVA gradually increases before stabilizing near 14%. This is mainly due to some legitimate vehicles mimicking the motion patterns of attackers, which results in an overestimation of their malicious scores. For reference, TIM yields a slightly higher FBR of approximately 16% under comparable conditions. These observations collectively verify that TA-RVA consistently delivers more accurate trust evaluations than TIM. In summary, TA-RVA demonstrates strong trust enforcement capabilities throughout its deployment.

4.4.3 Network Performance

To comprehensively evaluate network performance, two core metrics are adopted: average delay and packet delivery ratio. The former reflects the average transmission time required for data packets to reach their designated destinations. The latter evaluates transmission efficiency by calculating the proportion of successfully received packets relative to the total packets generated during the simulation. A total of 1000 simulation iterations are conducted, and the average values of both metrics are computed across these episodes. The obtained results are then compared with those from the baseline CACA approach to demonstrate the performance gains offered by the proposed framework.

According to the results presented in Fig. 4.6a, b, TA-RVA achieves comparable performance in terms of average delay and packet delivery ratio when evaluated against the reference CACA model. This consistency stems from TA-RVA's design,

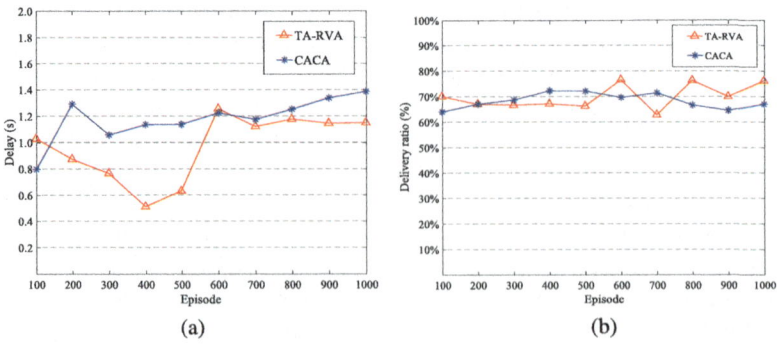

Fig. 4.6 Network performance for different episodes. (**a**) Average delay. (**b**) Average delivery ratio

which incorporates a variety of network-level constraints to preserve key QoS attributes. Hence, we infer that integrating the proposed MTD mechanism does not significantly compromise QoS and ensures reliable system behavior within a tolerable performance range.

4.5 Conclusion

This study introduces an intelligent MTD framework composed of two core components: PPO-OCM and TA-RVA. To begin with, the dynamic reconfiguration process of RSUs is formulated as a MDP, enabling the application of DRL to derive optimal strategies. Subsequently, a trust evaluation model is constructed to detect malicious vehicles under multiple operational constraints. Comprehensive simulation experiments are conducted to validate the performance and security benefits of the proposed solution.

In future work, we intend to extend our framework by incorporating considerations of flow table storage limitations and communication latency. Moreover, future research will explore emerging security threats associated with integrating SDN into the IoV.

References

1. Zhang, Q., Yu, K., Guo, Z., Garg, S., Rodrigues, J.J.P.C., Hassan, M.M., Guizani, M.: Graph neural network-driven traffic forecasting for the connected internet of vehicles. IEEE Trans. Netw. Sci. Eng. **9**(5), 3015–3027 (2021)
2. Hu, C., Fan, W., Zeng, E., Hang, Z., Wang, F., Qi, L., Bhuiyan, M.Z.A.: Digital twin-assisted real-time traffic data prediction method for 5g-enabled internet of vehicles. IEEE Trans. Indust. Inform. **18**(4), 2811–2819 (2021)
3. Mekki, T., Jabri, I., Rachedi, A., Chaari, L.: Software-defined networking in vehicular networks: a survey. Trans. Emerg. Telecommun. Technol. **33**(10), e4265 (2022)
4. Sharma, N., Chauhan, N., Chand, N., Awasthi, L.K.: Secure authentication and session key management scheme for internet of vehicles. Trans. Emerg. Telecommun. Technol. **33**(5), e4451 (2022)
5. Mejri, M.N., Ben-Othman, J.: Gdvan: a new greedy behavior attack detection algorithm for vanets. IEEE Trans. Mob. Comput. **16**(3), 759–771 (2016)
6. de Biasi, G., Vieira, L.F.M., Loureiro, A.A.F.: Sentinel: defense mechanism against ddos flooding attack in software defined vehicular network. In: 2018 IEEE International Conference on Communications (ICC), pp. 1–6. IEEE (2018)
7. Hbaieb, A., Ayed, S., Chaari, L.: A survey of trust management in the internet of vehicles. Comput. Netw. **203**, 108558 (2022)
8. Xia, H., Zhang, S.-s., Li, Y., Pan, Z.-k., Peng, X., Cheng, X.-z.: An attack-resistant trust inference model for securing routing in vehicular ad hoc networks. IEEE Trans. Veh. Technol. **68**(7), 7108–7120 (2019)
9. Nigam, R., Sharma, D.K., Jain, S., Bhardwaj, K.K., Banyal, S.: Ai-enabled trust-based routing protocol for social opportunistic iot networks. Trans. Emerg. Telecommun. Technol. **35**(4), e4330 (2024)

10. Li, J., Xue, Z., Li, C., Liu, M.: Rted-sd: a real-time edge detection scheme for sybil ddos in the internet of vehicles. IEEE Access **9**, 11296–11305 (2021)
11. Zhang, J., Bhuiyan, M.Z.A., Yang, X., Wang, T., Xu, X., Hayajneh, T., Khan, F.: Anticoncealer: reliable detection of adversary concealed behaviors in edgeai-assisted iot. IEEE Internet Things J. **9**(22), 22184–22193 (2021)
12. Zhang, T., Kuang, X., Zhou, Z., Gao, H., Xu, C.: An intelligent route mutation mechanism against mixed attack based on security awareness. In: 2019 IEEE Global Communications Conference (GLOBECOM), pp. 1–6. IEEE (2019)
13. Xu, C., Zhang, T., Kuang, X., Zhou, Z., Yu, S.: Context-aware adaptive route mutation scheme: a reinforcement learning approach. IEEE Internet Things J. **8**(17), 13528–13541 (2021)
14. Zhang, T., Xu, C., Zhang, B., Kuang, X., Wang, Y., Yang, S., Muntean, G.-M.: Dq-rm: deep reinforcement learning-based route mutation scheme for multimedia services. In: 2020 International Wireless Communications and Mobile Computing (IWCMC), pp. 291–296. IEEE (2020)
15. Duan, Q., Al-Shaer, E., Xie, J.: Range and topology mutation based wireless agility. In: Proceedings of the 7th ACM Workshop on Moving Target Defense, pp. 59–67 (2020)
16. Zhou, Y., Cheng, G., Zhao, Y., Chen, Z., Jiang, S.: Toward proactive and efficient ddos mitigation in iiot systems: a moving target defense approach. IEEE Trans. Indust. Inform. **18**(4), 2734–2744 (2021)
17. Soussi, W., Christopoulou, M., Xilouris, G., Gür, G.: Moving target defense as a proactive defense element for beyond 5g. IEEE Commun. Stand. Mag. **5**(3), 72–79 (2021)
18. Lu, X. Xiao, L., Xu, T., Zhao, Y., Tang, Y., Zhuang, W.: Reinforcement learning based phy authentication for vanets. IEEE Trans. Veh. Technol. **69**(3), 3068–3079 (2020)
19. De Moura, L., Bjørner, N.: Satisfiability modulo theories: introduction and applications. Commun. ACM **54**(9), 69–77 (2011)
20. Bai, F., Sadagopan, N., Helmy, A.: The important framework for analyzing the impact of mobility on performance of routing protocols for adhoc networks. Ad Hoc Netw. **1**(4), 383–403 (2003)
21. Siddiqui, A.J., Boukerche, A.: On the impact of ddos attacks on software-defined internet-of-vehicles control plane. In: 2018 14th International Wireless Communications & Mobile Computing Conference (IWCMC), pp. 1284–1289. IEEE (2018)
22. Sahoo, K.S., Puthal, D., Tiwary, M., Rodrigues, J.J.P.C., Sahoo, B., Dash, R.: An early detection of low rate ddos attack to sdn based data center networks using information distance metrics. Future Gener. Comput. Syst. **89**, 685–697 (2018)
23. Yuan, B., Zou, D., Yu, S., Jin, H., Qiang, W., Shen, J.: Defending against flow table overloading attack in software-defined networks. IEEE Trans. Serv. Comput. **12**(2), 231–246 (2016)
24. Tao, J., Zhu, L., Wang, X., He, J., Liu, Y.: Rsu deployment scheme with power control for highway message propagation in vanets. In: 2014 IEEE Global Communications Conference, pp. 169–174. IEEE (2014)
25. He, T., Bao, J., Li, R., Ruan, S., Li, Y., Song, L., He, H., Zheng, Y.: What is the human mobility in a new city: transfer mobility knowledge across cities. In: Proceedings of the Web Conference 2020, pp. 1355–1365 (2020)
26. Li, F., Song, X., Chen, H., Li, X., Wang, Y.: Hierarchical routing for vehicular ad hoc networks via reinforcement learning. IEEE Trans. Veh. Technol. **68**(2), 1852–1865 (2018)
27. De Moura, L., Bjørner, N.: Z3: an efficient smt solver. In: International conference on Tools and Algorithms for the Construction and Analysis of Systems, pp. 337–340. Springer, Berlin (2008)
28. Haadi Jafarian, J., Al-Shaer, E., Duan, Q.: An effective address mutation approach for disrupting reconnaissance attacks. IEEE Trans. Inf. Forensics Secur. **10**(12), 2562–2577 (2015)
29. He, Y., Zhang, M., Yang, X., Sun, Q.T., Luo, J., Yu, Y.: The intelligent offense and defense mechanism of internet of vehicles based on the differential game-ip hopping. IEEE Access **8**, 115217–115227 (2020)
30. The simulation of urban mobility. http://sumo.sourceforge.net. Accessed 4 March 2022
31. The ns-3 network simulator. https://www.nsnam.org. Accessed 4 March 2022

References

32. The netanim. https://www.nsnam.org/wiki/NetAnim_3.108. Accessed 4 March 2022
33. Gawłowicz, P., Zubow, A.: ns3-gym: extending openai gym for networking research (2018). arXiv preprint arXiv:1810.03943
34. Wong, W., Thakur, A., Gary Chan, S.-H.: An approximation algorithm for ap association under user migration cost constraint. In: IEEE INFOCOM 2016-The 35th Annual IEEE International Conference on Computer Communications, pp. 1–9. IEEE (2016)
35. Fortino, G., Messina, F., Rosaci, D., Sarné, G.M.L., Savaglio, C.: A trust-based team formation framework for mobile intelligence in smart factories. IEEE Trans. Indust. Inform. **16**(9), 6133–6142 (2020)

Chapter 5
AI-Driven Moving Target Defense for VANETs: Route Mutation via Multiagent Reinforcement Learning

Abstract VANETs are highly vulnerable to packet drop and route manipulation attacks due to their inherently distributed nature and rapidly changing topology. Traditional security mechanisms, such as multi-path routing and trust-based forwarding, are limited in practical deployment: the former introduces significant energy overhead, while the latter depends on complex and often unreliable trust evaluations. In this work, we introduce a novel MTD strategy enhanced by AI to dynamically and intelligently adapt routing paths, thereby increasing the uncertainty and cost for adversaries. Specifically, we design a Grid-based Extended Joint Action Learning framework (Grid-eJAL), which leverages MARL to implement an online and adaptive MTD policy tailored for VANETs. Unlike conventional route mutation schemes that rely on static topologies and centralized control, Grid-eJAL supports decentralized, real-time decision-making by enabling vehicles to share learned parameters, accelerating convergence without compromising autonomy. The physical region is partitioned into equal-sized grids, and the AI agent selects the next hop within the optimal grid based on minimum mobility angle and learned defense strategies. The theoretical foundations of Grid-eJAL ensure its convergence. Finally, comprehensive experiments demonstrate its superiority over advanced baseline methods in various adversarial scenarios.

Keywords Moving target defense · Route mutation · Cyber attack · Multi-agent reinforcement learning

5.1 Introduction

5.1.1 Motivations

VANETs [1] are large-scale, dynamic distributed systems composed of heterogeneous nodes. Enabled by V2V and V2I communications, VANETs support real-time alert dissemination, collision avoidance, multimedia services, and other safety-critical applications [2]. However, due to their high mobility, open wireless channels, and decentralized architecture, VANETs are inherently vulnerable to various cyber threats, which may lead to traffic disruptions, physical accidents, or privacy violations [3].

One of the most prominent threats in VANETs is the packet drop attack, where compromised nodes deliberately discard transit packets to disrupt communication. To address such attacks, prior works have primarily explored secure routing strategies, including multi-path routing [4–6] and trust-based routing [7, 8]. In multi-path routing, packets are split into multiple shares and sent via diverse paths to improve resilience; however, this incurs significant communication and energy overhead due to redundant transmissions. Trust-based routing attempts to select reliable nodes based on historical behavior, yet establishing accurate trust metrics is highly challenging in dynamic and adversarial environments [9].

These limitations motivate the exploration of AI-driven MTD mechanisms, which can dynamically and proactively alter network configurations, routing paths, or system parameters to increase attack uncertainty and reduce the adversary's success probability. Compared with static defense strategies, AI-MTD offers adaptivity and decision-making capabilities that are crucial in evolving VANET threat landscapes.

5.1.2 Challenges

MTD [10, 11] has recently emerged as a promising paradigm to enhance network security by introducing dynamic and unpredictable changes to system configurations, such as IP addresses, port numbers, and routing paths. Within this framework, RM techniques have been proposed to periodically alter communication paths, thereby increasing the complexity for attackers to perform reconnaissance or execute targeted attacks [12–15]. For instance, Kang et al. [16] demonstrate that static traffic patterns lead to the formation of critical nodes, which become prime targets for reconnaissance, eavesdropping, and DDoS attacks. RM mitigates this by rerouting traffic to avoid such predictable points of failure. Despite its potential, existing RM strategies face critical challenges when applied to VANETs. Most traditional RM schemes are designed for static or quasi-static network topologies, and thus fail to accommodate the highly dynamic nature of VANETs. Moreover, current RM solutions often rely on centralized control architectures. As the network scales, these centralized controllers become bottlenecks and single points of failure, making them vulnerable to overload and targeted compromise. These limitations highlight the necessity for decentralized and intelligent RM mechanisms tailored to VANET environments. In this paper, AI-based MTD offers a compelling alternative. By leveraging machine learning and real-time situational awareness, AI-MTD can dynamically adapt routing strategies in a distributed manner, enabling more robust, scalable, and context-aware defense against evolving adversarial tactics in mobile environments.

5.1 Introduction

To tackle the above limitations, we introduce a novel Grid-based Extended Joint Action LearningGrid-based Grid-eJAL algorithm, a novel framework for deploying AI-driven MTD strategies in VANETs. Departing from conventional RM approaches, this method synergizes RM with MARL to proactively avoid routes involving potentially malicious infrastructure. At the core of this strategy lies an enhanced version of Joint Action Learning, referred to as extended JAL (eJAL), which operates in a real-time, adaptive fashion, empowering vehicles to autonomously determine secure, context-sensitive routes without requiring prior insight into the network topology. MARL is particularly promising in distributed decision-making scenarios, owing to its capacity to derive optimal policies through localized interactions and delayed rewards [17, 18]. These characteristics render it well-suited for highly dynamic, large-scale environments with incomplete observability, typical of VANETs, where centralized orchestration is either inefficient or impractical, and agent behavior evolves continuously.

This paper highlights the following key contributions:

1. To our knowledge, this study presents the pioneering AI-driven MTD framework that leverages a real-time adaptive MARL-based mechanism to facilitate intelligent routing path adjustments in VANETs. The proposed scheme supports secure and robust data transmission by proactively steering away from routes prone to packet loss attacks.
2. In response to the routing complexity caused by dynamic vehicular mobility, we segment the geographic space into uniformly sized grid units. The forwarding behavior of each vehicle is characterized through a MDP, wherein the system state includes the vehicle's current location, target grid, and the remaining time-to-live (TTL) of the packet. The decision-making process involves choosing an adjacent grid that offers the highest probability of secure transmission, enabling the system to be both analytically manageable and performance-optimized.
3. We enhance the standard MARL model by introducing an improved framework named eJAL, which permits participating vehicles (agents) to exchange Q-values, thereby accelerating convergence and strengthening adaptability. This allows the system to acquire secure routing policies more efficiently in real-time scenarios. Upon determining the destination grid, a refined relay selection strategy based on the minimum-angle principle is employed to pinpoint the most dependable forwarding node, thus improving the likelihood of successful delivery.
4. To validate the proposed Grid-eJAL framework, we conduct both theoretical analyses focusing on complexity and convergence and comprehensive simulation-based evaluations. The results indicate that Grid-eJAL achieves notable advancements over existing methods in three critical dimensions: defense capability, communication efficiency, and convergence behavior. Specifically, the framework attains an approximate defense success rate of 99% when countering diverse packet drop attack scenarios.

5.1.3 Related Work

To ensure secure routing in wireless ad hoc networks, prior research has primarily focused on multi-path and trust-based routing schemes. Multi-path routing aims to enhance robustness by splitting packets into multiple shares and transmitting them via different routes, as demonstrated by TMPAR [4], and other frameworks leveraging SDN-based hybrid architectures [5] or stochastic processes [6]. However, these solutions introduce considerable communication and energy overhead, especially when redundant shares are transmitted or when concurrent paths lead to increased MAC-layer contention. Trust-based routing, on the other hand, attempts to select reliable nodes based on observed behavior or inferred reputation. Representative works include, ActiveTrust [9] and other trust modeling frameworks [7]. Although such approaches can improve security, their effectiveness relies on the availability and accuracy of trust information, which is often infeasible to maintain in highly dynamic and adversarial environments like VANETs.

In recent years, MTD, particularly in the form of RM, has emerged as a prominent direction in network security research. Duan et al. [10] introduced one of the earliest RM frameworks, termed Random Route Mutation (RRM). Building upon RRM, Gillani et al. [11] designed a strategy that unpredictably alters the exposure of key network resources to disrupt adversarial reconnaissance. Zhang et al. [12] advanced this line of work by employing hypothesis testing to guide the selection of mutation strategies against malicious scanning behavior. In another study, Duan et al. [13] developed a proactive RM mechanism that aims to obscure an attacker's understanding of critical network links. Additionally, our previous research [14, 15, 19] proposed reinforcement learning-based MTD solutions, which significantly enhanced overall defense effectiveness. Despite their benefits, these RM strategies often assume relatively stable network structures and therefore struggle to cope with the frequent topology changes and real-time constraints inherent to VANETs, limiting their practical applicability in such dynamic environments.

Parallel to this, RL has proven successful in optimizing routing decisions under dynamic conditions in VANETs. Protocols like QGrid [20], intersection-aware Q-learning [21], and deep RL-based trust frameworks [22] significantly improve delivery efficiency and adaptability. However, these works primarily target performance optimization and do not explicitly address adversarial threats such as packet drop attacks.

To tackle both adaptivity and security in a distributed manner, MARL has attracted growing interest due to its capability of collaborative learning via experience sharing and joint decision-making [23, 24]. MARL's decentralized nature makes it a promising candidate for intelligent MTD in VANETs. Nevertheless, to the best of our knowledge, no prior work has explored an online and adaptive MARL algorithm tailored for route mutation to defend against packet drop attacks in VANET scenarios. This paper addresses this gap by proposing a scalable, AI-based MTD approach designed specifically for dynamic vehicular environments.

5.2 Model Formulation on the End Layer

5.2.1 Network Model

As shown in Fig. 5.1, we investigate a VANET scenario comprising N vehicles, M base stations (BSs), and L RSUs. This network is modeled as an undirected graph $\mathbb{G} = (\mathbb{V}, \mathbb{E})$, where $\mathbb{V}$ denotes the complete set of nodes v_i ($1 \leq i \leq N + M + L$), including all participating vehicles, BSs, and RSUs, and $\mathbb{E}$ represents the wireless communication links e_{ij} that interconnect node pairs v_i and v_j within $\mathbb{V}$. For notational clarity, we use v_i^V to indicate vehicle nodes and v_i^R to refer to RSUs. In this setting, the routing task from a source node v_s to a destination node v_d involves selecting a path that sequentially passes through a series of intermediate nodes and their associated wireless edges.

Vehicle movement within the specified area follows the Manhattan grid mobility model [25]. BSs and RSUs are evenly deployed throughout the area of interest. While RSUs primarily act as relays to assist in message forwarding, BSs typically function as service-providing endpoints. To reach nodes outside the direct transmission range, multi-hop routing is employed.

Each vehicle is equipped with GPS modules or onboard sensors, enabling it to determine its current location, heading, and velocity in real time. We assume the availability of GPS refinement technologies [26–28], which enhance the precision of position estimation. Alternatively, RSUs can broadcast directional and positional information to vehicles, while speed is measured using internal sensors [29]. The system supports both V2V and V2I communication modes, allowing for flexible

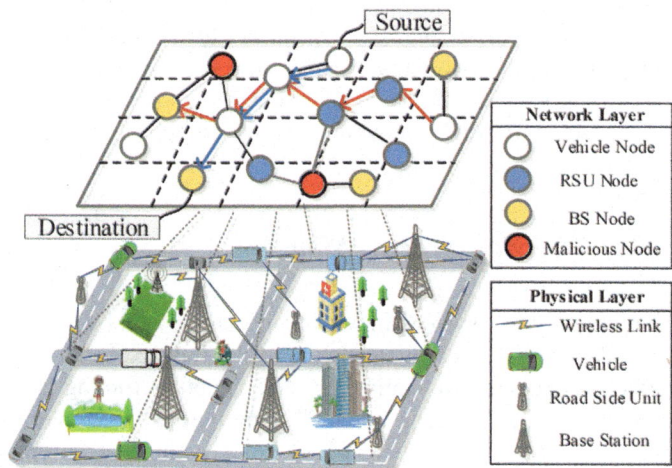

Fig. 5.1 An example case of hierarchical routing in VANETs

data exchange among different types of nodes. Moreover, vehicles periodically share HELLO messages via V2V links to inform neighboring nodes of their own location, trajectory, and velocity.

5.2.2 Threat Model

To begin with, following the assumptions made in prior works such as [9, 30], we assume that link-layer security is ensured through cryptographic mechanisms. Specifically, each communication link along an end-to-end route is protected by symmetric encryption. As a result, only the intended recipient can decipher the transmitted messages, rendering eavesdropping over the wireless medium ineffective for unauthorized parties.

Furthermore, the attacker may either be an external entity residing within the communication range of the VANET, or it may escalate to an internal threat by initially breaching one or more RSUs. Once compromised, these RSUs act as malicious insiders. When acting as an external adversary, the attacker primarily launches DDoS attacks targeting selected RSUs, thereby disrupting packet forwarding at those points. In this paper, we focus on the more plausible scenario where only RSUs are vulnerable to compromise. This assumption is justified by the fact that RSUs are typically deployed in publicly accessible locations and exhibit weaker security protections compared to BSs [31].

Lastly, regardless of whether the threat originates from inside or outside the network, any routing path that involves a compromised RSU may experience packet loss, occurring with a probability denoted by $\mathcal{P}_d$. When this probability reaches 100%, the resulting behavior constitutes a black hole attack (BHA) [9], characterized by the complete suppression of packet forwarding. In contrast, when $\mathcal{P}_d$ is lower than 100%, the adversary engages in a grey hole attack (GHA) [32], selectively discarding packets. To evade detection, the compromised nodes falsely report successful packet transmission while covertly dropping a portion of the data.

5.2.3 Markov Decision Process Model

We consider a slotted-time system in which the entire timeline is divided into uniform intervals of duration ΔT, with each time slot indexed by $t \in \{0, 1, 2, \cdots\}$. To enable effective message dissemination and adaptive routing decisions, the VANET is modeled as a multi-agent system. The participating vehicles are denoted by the set $\{v_1^V, \cdots, v_N^V\}$. Each vehicle v_i^V operates within the forwarding phase according to a MDP formulation. The core elements of this model are defined as follows:

5.2 Model Formulation on the End Layer

5.2.3.1 Network State Space and Observation

In this work, we partition the target region into equally sized square units, referred to as grids. Suppose the entire area consists of $H \times H$ grids, and let L_t represent the number of packets scheduled for forwarding in the next time slot. At each time slot t, the overall network state perceived by a vehicle v_i^V is denoted as $S_t = \{s_{xy}^c, s_{mn}^d, s_L^{ttl}\}$, where s_{xy}^c ($1 \leq x, y \leq H$) identifies the grid currently occupied by the vehicle, s_{mn}^d ($1 \leq m, n \leq H$) denotes the destination grid associated with the ongoing transmission, and s_L^{ttl} is the TTL value of the L_t packets awaiting forwarding, all of which are assumed to belong to the same communication session. The set $\mathbb{S}$ defines the entire network state space, encompassing every feasible configuration that a vehicle may encounter throughout its routing process. Due to the localized nature of signalling exchanges, each vehicle is only capable of observing its neighbors residing within the same grid cell.

5.2.3.2 Action Space

In the proposed scheme, the initial decision step involves identifying the neighboring grid where the subsequent forwarding node should reside. During the learning phase, the action taken by vehicle v_i^V at time slot t is denoted as $A_t = \{a_k\}$, where a_k ($1 \leq k \leq 8$) corresponds to the selection of one of the adjacent grids. Since each grid is surrounded by at most eight neighbors, the value of k indexes up to eight possible directions. The vehicle's action space, represented by $\mathbb{A}$, encompasses the complete set of selectable actions. Following the grid selection, vehicle v_i^V further chooses a specific relay node, either another vehicle or RSU, within the chosen grid to serve as the next hop in the routing path.

5.2.3.3 State Transition

Based on the defined network state, state transitions are predominantly influenced by vehicle movement and variations in TTL values. In particular, when a vehicle moves from one grid cell to another, the system updates its state to capture the vehicle's new location. Moreover, changes in TTL, either through countdown or reset, also play a key role in driving the evolution of the network state across time slots.

5.2.3.4 Reward Function

Given that the data transmission speed in vehicular networks significantly exceeds vehicle mobility, we assume that each forwarding operation along a transmission path can be completed within a single time slot. Consequently, the corresponding reward signals are also received by the forwarding nodes within the same slot. At each time step, every vehicle is assigned an immediate reward that reflects both the prevailing network conditions and the action it selects. To quantify the effectiveness of routing behavior, we define the reward $\mathcal{R}_{t,i}$ received by vehicle v_i^V at time slot t as a composite of three components: grid-level destination awareness, packet loss penalty, and distance-based progression toward the destination. The reward formulation is given as:

$$\mathcal{R}_{t,i} = \mathcal{R}_{t,i}^s + \mathcal{R}_{t,i}^l + \mathcal{R}_{t,i}^d. \tag{5.1}$$

The first term, denoted as $\mathcal{R}_{t,i}^s$, captures the degree of spatial relevance between the vehicle's selected next-hop grid and the final destination. A fixed reward C^+ is granted when the destination node is located within the chosen neighboring grid; otherwise, the vehicle receives no reward. This can be formally defined as:

$$\mathcal{R}_{t,i}^s = \begin{cases} C^+, & \text{if destination resides in the selected next-hop grid,} \\ 0, & \text{Otherwise.} \end{cases} \tag{5.2}$$

The second term, $\mathcal{R}_{t,i}^l$, imposes a penalty in case of packet delivery failure. If the destination does not acknowledge the packet in a timely manner, indicative of packet loss, then each intermediate node (including RSUs and vehicles) along the path incurs a negative reward scaled by the path length. This is formally expressed as:

$$\mathcal{R}_{t,i}^l = \begin{cases} C^- \Psi_t, & \text{if transmitted packet is lost,} \\ 0, & \text{otherwise,} \end{cases} \tag{5.3}$$

where C^- is a fixed penalty value and Ψ_t denotes the number of hops taken so far, which can be inferred from the TTL field in the current state. Packet losses may arise due to several factors, such as malicious packet dropping, TTL expiration, or wireless transmission errors.

The third term, $\mathcal{R}_{t,i}^d$, evaluates whether the forwarding decision brings the data closer to the destination. This metric helps prevent routing loops and accelerates packet delivery. If the chosen next hop decreases the Euclidean distance to the destination, a positive reward is assigned; otherwise, a penalty is applied. The formulation is as follows:

$$\mathcal{R}_{t,i}^d = \sigma_i \left(\mathcal{D}(v_{i-1}, v_d) - \mathcal{D}(v_i, v_d) \right), \tag{5.4}$$

where σ_i denotes a weighting factor for vehicle v_i^V, $\mathcal{D}(v_{i-1}, v_d)$ denotes the distance between the previous hop and the destination, and $\mathcal{D}(v_i, v_d)$ denotes the current node's distance to the destination node.

5.3 Detailed Design

JAL [33] extends the traditional Q-learning framework by incorporating joint actions among multiple agents. Given that packet forwarding in VANETs inherently relies on inter-vehicle collaboration, we adapt the Q-learning update mechanism accordingly. Specifically, once a forwarding vehicle selects a neighboring grid, the packet effectively transitions to the corresponding grid in the next time slot. Since vehicle mobility governs the evolution of network state, we reinterpret the next state S_{t+1} in Eq. (5.7) as the packet's subsequent location state, rather than the individual vehicle's. This adjustment aligns the Q-value update process more closely with the objective of efficient packet delivery, thereby enhancing routing effectiveness in dynamic vehicular environments.

As shown in Fig. 5.2, we present a simplified case to demonstrate how the modified Q-value update mechanism helps mitigate the influence of malicious nodes during packet forwarding. For clarity, we assume that each network state is occupied

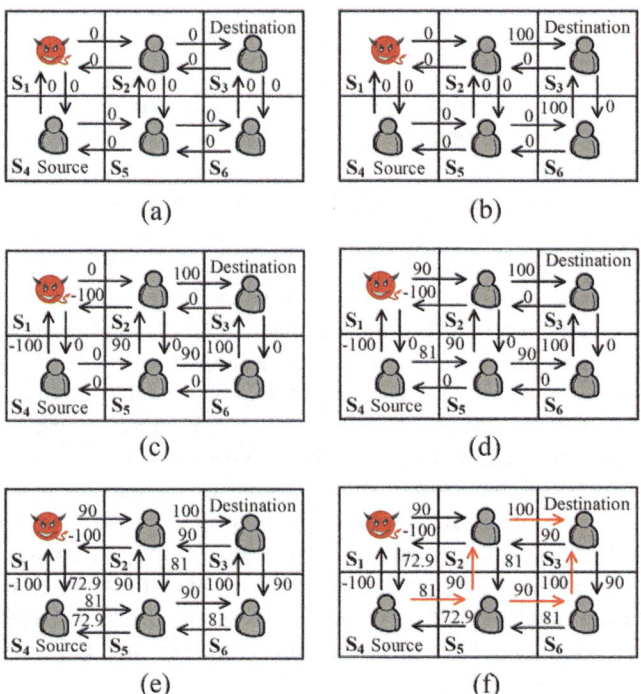

Fig. 5.2 Illustration of the reinforcement learning process in a grid-based multi-agent scenario. (**a**) shows the initial setup with the source node located in S_4, the destination in S_3, and a malicious agent positioned in S_1. (**b**), (**c**), and (**d**) sequentially show the Q-values update process based on agent actions and received rewards. (**e**) shows the stabilized Q-values after the learning process converges. (**f**) shows two viable routing paths in red that successfully circumvent the adversarial node. (**a**) The initial state. (**b**) An intermediate state I. (**c**) An intermediate state II. (**d**) An intermediate state III. (**e**) The final state. (**f**) Two feasible routes

by a single stationary agent, and that agents are capable of sharing Q-values with their neighbors. Arrows in the figure represent the forwarding decisions, i.e., the selection of neighboring grids for routing, and the associated Q-value is displayed above each arrow. For this example, we constrain the action set to four directions: up, down, left, and right. Given the assumption that each grid contains only one agent, we omit the intra-grid node selection process. The reward function is defined as follows: delivering a packet directly to the destination yields a positive reward of 100, forwarding to a malicious node incurs a penalty of -100, and all other forwarding actions receive a neutral reward of 0. The discount factor is set to $\gamma = 0.9$, and the learning rate is fixed at $\alpha = 1$. Suppose that grid S_3 hosts the destination. Then, agents in grids S_2 and S_6 can deliver packets to S_3 within a single hop. According to Eq. (5.8), the Q-values for these one-hop actions are updated to $Q^{(2)}(S_2, A_{2\to 3}) = 100$ and $Q^{(6)}(S_6, A_{6\to 3}) = 100$, as depicted in Fig. 5.2b. Next, consider the case where an agent in S_5 must forward a packet. It can choose to send it either to S_2 or S_6. The resulting Q-values are calculated as follows:

$$Q^{(5)}(S_5, A_{5\to 2}) = 0 + 0.9 \max\{-100, 100, 0\} = 90, \tag{5.5}$$

$$Q^{(5)}(S_5, A_{5\to 6}) = 0 + 0.9 \max\{0, 100\} = 90, \tag{5.6}$$

as illustrated in Fig. 5.2c. Q-values throughout the network are progressively updated using Eq. (5.8) until they reach convergence, that is, when the values become stable and no longer change with further iterations. Given a scenario where the source node is positioned at S_4 and the destination resides at S_3, two secure and effective routing paths emerge: $S_4 \to S_5 \to S_2 \to S_3$ and $S_4 \to S_5 \to S_6 \to S_3$. These attack-resilient paths are visually highlighted in red in Fig. 5.2f.

We now examine the stationarity characteristics of the vehicular environment. According to studies in [20, 34], vehicular trajectories exhibit high regularity, akin to human movement patterns, particularly in urban environments. In many cases, vehicles follow habitual routes, resulting in relatively stable mobility behaviors. However, some vehicles, such as taxis, may adopt unpredictable or stochastic motion strategies. In scenarios where vehicle mobility patterns remain constant, a sufficiently long training period allows agents to explore all reachable states due to the finite size of the state space. Once the Q-values converge, each agent learns the best action for every encountered state. On the other hand, if vehicles change their movement policies during the training phase, the learning process must restart in affected states, resulting in prolonged convergence. Nevertheless, such non-stationarity impacts only the learning time, not the eventual convergence itself.

5.3.1 Secure Grid Selection Based on Extended Joint Action Learning

In this subsection, we present an intelligent approach for selecting a secure neighboring grid for both vehicles and RSUs. Leveraging the grid-based structure

5.3 Detailed Design

of the network, we extend the classical JAL framework by proposing an improved variant, referred to as eJAL. The enhanced design of eJAL ensures scalability, as its state-action space remains compact and tractable regardless of the growth in the number of participating vehicles.

To facilitate cooperative learning, we design a communication protocol that allows vehicles to monitor the behavior of their peers and exchange Q-value information. All vehicles are assumed to operate cooperatively in forwarding packets from source to destination, with the common objective of maximizing long-term rewards. This cooperation is realized through the exchange of control messages over a shared communication channel with one-hop neighbors, a mechanism commonly adopted in related works [35]. When vehicle v_i^V seeks to query another vehicle v_j^V, it sends a request to retrieve statistics on action selections. Specifically, it retrieves the count $\mathcal{N}_{t,i}^{(j)}(A_t)$, which represents how often action A_t has been selected by v_j^V up to time t. This information-sharing process is decoupled from the action-selection mechanism and does not interfere with the environment, thereby maintaining the validity of the learning framework. Such communication strategies have been extensively explored in prior research [36, 37], with further studies addressing the scheduling of inter-vehicle communication in cooperative systems [38, 39].

Let v_i^V denote a vehicle currently holding a non-empty packet queue, and let $\mathcal{L}(v_i^V)$ represent the set of neighboring vehicles located within the same grid as v_i^V. For each vehicle $v_j^V \in \mathcal{L}(v_i^V)$, we define the probability that v_i^V selects action A_t at time slot t as follows:

$$P_{t,i}^{(j)}(A_t) = \mathcal{N}_{t,i}^{(j)}(A_t) \bigg/ \sum_{A_z \in \mathbb{A}} \mathcal{N}_{t,i}^{(j)}(A_z), \tag{5.7}$$

where $\sum_{A_z \in \mathbb{A}} \mathcal{N}_{t,i}^{(j)}(A_z)$ represents the total number of times vehicle v_j^V has executed actions from the available action space $\mathbb{A}$, as perceived by v_i^V. Utilizing this, v_i^V computes the normalized action selection probability across all its neighboring vehicles. The normalized probability that v_j^V selects action A_t is given by:

$$\overline{P}_{t,i}^{(j)}(A_t) = P_{t,i}^{(j)}(A_t) \bigg/ \sum_{v_l^V \in \mathcal{L}(v_i^V)} P_{t,i}^{(l)}(A_t), \tag{5.8}$$

where $\overline{P}_{t,i}^{(j)}(A_t)$ denotes the normalized probability that vehicle v_j^V selects action A_t at time t, as perceived by vehicle v_i^V.

At the end of each time slot, every vehicle shares its current Q-values with neighboring nodes residing in the same grid. Based on this information, vehicle v_i^V computes a joint Q-value estimation for action A_t by aggregating the Q-values of its neighbors, weighted by their normalized action probabilities:

$$\overline{Q}_t(A_t) = \sum_{v_j^V \in \mathcal{L}(v_i^V)} Q_{t,j}(S_t, A_t) \cdot \overline{P}_{t,i}^{(j)}(A_t), \quad (5.9)$$

where $\overline{Q}_t(A_t)$ denotes the collaboratively estimated Q-value associated with action A_t. Leveraging this aggregated estimate, vehicle v_i^V proceeds to update its own Q-value corresponding to the state-action pair (S_t, A_t) according to the following update rule:

$$Q_{t,i}(S_t, A_t) = (1 - \beta_t) Q_{t,i}(S_t, A_t) \\ + \beta_t \overline{Q}_t(A_t), \quad (5.10)$$

where β_t is the learning rate used to blend the previous estimate with the newly aggregated value. This cooperative communication mechanism significantly accelerates the learning process. In particular, when vehicle v_i^V enters a previously unvisited grid, it can leverage the joint Q-value estimates provided by neighbors to initialize its own Q-values, thus avoiding the inefficiency of learning solely through trial-and-error.

To enable adaptive control over the Q-value update rate, we introduce a time-varying parameter β_t, which is determined based on how frequently a vehicle has visited its current grid. The underlying intuition is that grids with fewer past visits warrant a higher update rate to accelerate learning in unfamiliar regions. To model this adaptive behavior, we use a sigmoid function to modulate the value of β_t. Let $Mt, i(S_t)$ represent the number of times vehicle v_i^V has traversed grid S_t prior to time slot t, which is locally calculated using the vehicle's recorded GPS history. In alignment with the Q-value sharing protocol, each vehicle also broadcasts its current $M_{t,i}(S_t)$ value to neighboring nodes at the end of each time slot. Upon receiving this information, vehicle v_i^V computes the average visit frequency across its neighbors:

$$\overline{M}_t(S_t) = \frac{1}{W} \sum_{j=1}^{W} M_{t,j}(S_t) \quad (5.11)$$

where W denotes the number of vehicles currently located within the same grid. The update rate β_t is then determined using a sigmoid-based function defined as follows:

$$\beta_t(S_t) = 1 \Big/ \left(1 + e^{-\left(\overline{M}_t(S_t) - M_{t,i}(S_t)\right)}\right). \quad (5.12)$$

When $\overline{M}_t(S_t)$ is larger than $M_{t,i}(S_t)$, β_t approaches 1, which indicates that vehicle v_i^V will update its Q-values more rapidly. Conversely, when $\overline{Mt}(S_t)$ is smaller than $Mt, i(S_t)$, β_t approaches 0, signaling that the Q-value update should occur more slowly.

5.3 Detailed Design

Next, we introduce two online algorithms, with their corresponding pseudo-codes detailed in Algorithms 5 and 4. A key feature of the proposed approach is that it operates entirely in real-time and does not rely on any offline training stage. Specifically, Algorithm 5 is tailored for vehicles employing the eJAL-based learning framework, whereas Algorithm 4 applies to standard RSUs that do not participate in the learning process. The behaviors and knowledge of malicious RSUs have been discussed in the threat model.

For vehicular agents, as described in Algorithm 5, mobility enables them to explore diverse network states. The learning rate is defined as $\alpha = 1/\tau$, and the greedy factor is given by $\varepsilon = \delta^\tau$, where $\tau = \lceil t/\xi \rceil$ and ξ is a predefined constant. First, both the Q-value matrix Q and the packet buffer L_p are initialized to zero (lines 1–2). Each vehicle begins from an initial state and traverses multiple network states over T time slots, forming one complete episode (lines 3–6). To manage data traffic, each vehicle maintains a local queue that stores both received and newly generated packets (lines 8–10). Within each episode, vehicles determine the forwarding direction by applying an ε-greedy strategy to select a next-hop grid (lines 13–17). They then forward L_t packets, where L_t denotes the number of packets transmitted, and record the associated rewards (lines 19–20). Following packet delivery, vehicles compute the normalized action probabilities and aggregate neighboring Q-values to form a joint estimate, which is subsequently used to refine their own Q-values (line 21). Finally, Q-value updates are performed using the Bellman update rule (line 22).

For standard RSUs, as described in Algorithm 4, learning is not performed locally. Instead, these nodes obtain the joint estimated Q-values from vehicles residing within the same grid. This design is reasonable since RSUs remain stationary and do not experience state transitions. Sharing the joint estimated Q-values from vehicles helps RSUs effectively forward packets. Like vehicles, RSUs maintain a packet buffer to temporarily store incoming data (lines 4–6). During each episode, if the buffer is not empty, the RSU selects the next-hop grid by identifying the action with the highest associated Q-value (lines 7–8). It then proceeds to forward L_t packets, where L_t denotes the volume of packets transmitted in that time slot (line 9). Subsequently, the RSU calculates the normalized action probability and the joint Q-value estimate using the same approach adopted by vehicles (lines 10–12). Finally, it updates its local Q-value entries based on the aggregated feedback (line 13).

After determining the optimal next-hop grid using either Algorithm 5 or 4, the actual selection of a relay node within that grid must account for three potential situations:

- Case 1: When the target grid contains available nodes (vehicles and/or RSUs), vehicle v_i^V forwards the packet to a chosen node based on a predefined relay selection policy.
- Case 2: If the optimal grid lacks both vehicles and RSUs, v_i^V will fall back to an alternative suboptimal grid and reattempt the forwarding decision following the same selection strategy as in Case 1.

Algorithm 5 Enhanced joint action learning for grid-based routing mutation (per vehicle v_i^V)

1: Set hyperparameters: learning rate $\alpha = 1/\tau$, discount factor γ, exploration rate $\varepsilon = \delta^\tau$, and update term β_t.
2: Define constants ξ, γ, and δ; initialize the Q-value table to zeros, and assign packet buffer $L_p \leftarrow 0$.
3: **for** each episode index h in 1 to H **do**
4:     Choose an initial state S_0 randomly to begin the episode.
5:     **for** each time step t from 1 to T **do**
6:         Observe the current environment state $S_t \in \mathbb{S}$.
7:         **if** n_t packets are newly generated or received **then**
8:             Update the buffer size as $L_p \leftarrow L_p + n_t$.
9:         **end if**
10:        **if** $L_p > 0$ **then**
11:           Draw a sample p from the uniform distribution $\mathcal{U}(0, 1)$.
12:           Proceed to determine the next-hop grid node using the following rule:
13:           **if** $p \leq \varepsilon$ **then**
14:              Action A_t is picked randomly with uniform probability.
15:           **else**
16:              Select the action that yields the maximum expected return: $A_t = \arg\max_{A_z} Q(S_t, A_z)$.
17:           **end if**
18:           Execute A_t to forward L_t packets; reduce buffer: $L_p \leftarrow L_p - L_t$.
19:           Obtain the immediate reward signal $\mathcal{R}_{t,i}$.
20:           Use Eq. (5.9) to Eq. (5.11) to compute $P_{t,i}^{(j)}(A_t)$, $\overline{P}_{t,i}^{(j)}(A_t)$, and $\overline{Q}_t(A_t)$.
21:           Update joint Q-value using:

$$\beta_t(S_t) = \frac{1}{1 + \exp\left(-\left[\overline{\mathcal{M}_t}(S_t) - \mathcal{M}_{t,i}(S_t)\right]\right)}.$$

$$Q_{t,i}(S_t, A_t) = (1 - \beta_t(S_t)) \cdot Q_{t,i}(S_t, A_t) + \beta_t(S_t) \cdot \overline{Q}_t(A_t).$$

22:           Then apply the Bellman update with:

$$Q_{t+1,i}(S_t, A_t) = (1 - \alpha) Q_{t,i}(S_t, A_t) + \alpha \left[\mathcal{R}_{t,i} + \gamma \cdot \max_{A_z} Q_{t,i}(S_t', A_z)\right].$$

23:        **end if**
24:     **end for**
25: **end for**

- Case 3: In situations where no neighboring grids host eligible relay nodes, the vehicle v_i^V temporarily holds the packet and postpones forwarding until future transmission opportunities become available.

5.3 Detailed Design

Algorithm 6 Grid-based forwarding protocol for route mutation at RSU v_j^R

1: Initialize Q-table as all-zero matrix; set packet counter $L_p \leftarrow 0$.
2: **for** each episode $h = 1$ to H **do**
3:     **for** each time step $t = 1$ to T **do**
4:         **if** n_t new packets are observed **then**
5:             Buffer is increased: $L_p \leftarrow L_p + n_t$.
6:         **end if**
7:         **if** $L_p > 0$ **then**
8:             Identify the optimal grid cell for next-hop relay via:

$$A_t = \arg\max_{A_z} Q(S_t, A_z).$$

9:             Take action A_t, dispatch L_t packets; update buffer: $L_p \leftarrow L_p - L_t$.
10:            Receive immediate feedback $\mathcal{R}_{t,j}$.
11:            Use Eq. (5.9) to retrieve $P_{t,i}^{(j)}(A_t)$;
12:            Apply Eq. (5.10) to estimate $\overline{P}_{t,i}^{(j)}(A_t)$;
13:            Compute $\overline{Q}_t(A_t)$ via Eq. (5.11).
14:            With $\overline{Q}_t(A_t)$, update local Q-value table:

$$Q_{t,j}(S_t, A_t) \leftarrow \overline{Q}_t(A_t).$$

15:         **end if**
16:     **end for**
17: **end for**

5.3.2 Node Selection Strategy Inside Secure Grid

While Algorithms 5 and 4 enable the identification of the optimal next-hop grid, the problem of choosing an appropriate relay node within that grid remains unresolved. In VANETs, packet loss may occur due to *departure loss*, a situation where the sender exits the receiver's communication range before transmission completes. To address this challenge and enhance transmission reliability, we introduce a relay node selection scheme informed by the underlying vehicular mobility model. The core objective of this strategy is to reduce the risk of departure loss and thereby improve the probability of successful data delivery.

Let $\mathbb{V}_t^{(i)} = \{v_1, v_2, \cdots, v_q\}$ represent the set of q candidate relay nodes located within the next-hop grid selected by vehicle v_i at time t. The spatial positions of the source and destination vehicles, v_s and v_d, are given by (x_s, y_s) and (x_d, y_d), respectively. The coordinates of a potential relay node $v_j (1 \leq j \leq q)$ are represented as (x_j, y_j). In the environments modeled by the Manhattan mobility pattern, vehicles generally maintain linear motion along the grid-like road structure, changing direction only at intersections. As such, the motion of node v_j is described by a movement vector $\vec{m_j} = (m_{x_j}, m_{y_j})$, where m_{x_j} and m_{y_j} denote the velocity components along the x- and y-axes, respectively. To capture the directional relationship between the candidate node and the destination, we define a positional vector $\overrightarrow{O_j O_d} = (x_d - x_j, y_d - y_j)$ from node v_j to v_d. To assess how well the movement vector aligns with the geographical vector, we employ an angle-based metric, which quantifies the similarity between the two vectors. This metric is defined as:

$$\theta_j = \arccos \frac{\overrightarrow{m_j} \bullet \overrightarrow{O_j O_d}}{||\overrightarrow{m_j}|| \times ||\overrightarrow{O_j O_d}||}, \tag{5.13}$$

where "$\bullet$" denotes the vector dot product, and $|| \cdot ||$ represents the Euclidean norm. For RSUs, which remain fixed in position, the corresponding angle-based metric is constant and equals $90°$. A candidate node v_j is considered directionally favorable when its angle θ_j with respect to the destination is less than $90°$, indicating that it is moving closer to v_d, thereby increasing the possibility of successful packet delivery. By evaluating the angle metric for all potential relay nodes within the selected grid, the node with the smallest θ_j is chosen as the optimal forwarder, as it aligns best with the direction toward the destination and is thus most suitable for minimizing departure loss.

The detailed procedure of the minimum-angle-based relay selection strategy is illustrated in Algorithm 7. To prevent routing loops or infinite forwarding, each packet is assigned a TTL field, which is decremented by 1 after each hop. As long as the TTL remains positive, the packet continues to be forwarded following the proposed strategy; otherwise, it is dropped to avoid redundant transmission attempts (line 2). In scenarios where only a single vehicle or RSU exists within the selected next-hop grid, that node is directly designated as the relay (lines 3–5). In all other situations, the forwarding decision is made by comparing the angle-based metrics of all candidate nodes (lines 6–17).

Figure 5.3 presents a simplified example that demonstrates the operational flow of the Grid-eJAL algorithm. In this scenario, vehicle A is responsible for forwarding packets to a designated destination node F. Following the procedure outlined in Algorithm 5, A first identifies a secure next-hop grid while successfully bypassing the grid that contains the malicious node B. Subsequently, leveraging the minimum-angle selection strategy described in Algorithm 7, A selects vehicle C as the optimal relay. The packet is ultimately delivered to destination F, completing the routing path established by the Grid-eJAL framework.

We begin by evaluating the computational complexity of the proposed Grid-eJAL framework. Let $|\mathbb{S}|$ denote the total number of distinct network states, $|\mathbb{A}|$ denote the size of the action space, W be the number of neighboring vehicles within the same grid, q be the number of candidate vehicles or RSUs in the selected next-hop grid, K be the total number of epochs, and T the number of time slots per episode. Both Algorithms 5 and 4 require storage proportional to the state-action space, resulting in a space complexity of $O(|\mathbb{S}||\mathbb{A}|)$. As Algorithm 5 follows a value iteration paradigm, its worst-case time complexity is bounded by $O(KT(W+|\mathbb{A}|))$. In contrast, Algorithm 4, which omits action selection and learning, incurs a lower time complexity of $O(KTW)$. For Algorithm 7, which selects the optimal relay

5.4 Performance Evaluation and Analysis

Algorithm 7 Minimum angle selection strategy

1: Let $\{v_1, v_2, \cdots, v_q\}$ be the set of candidate vehicles and/or RSUs in the selected next-hop grid; $\theta_{min} = 180°$;
2: **if** TTL>0 **then**
3:    $TTL = TTL - 1$.
4:    **if** $q = 1$ **then**
5:       Forward the packet to the single available node.
6:    **else**
7:       **for** $j = 1, 2, \cdots, q$ **do**
8:          **if** v_j is vehicle **then**
9:             $\theta_j = \arccos \frac{\vec{m_j} \bullet \vec{O_j O_d}}{\|\vec{m_j}\| \times \|\vec{O_j O_d}\|}$.
10:         **else**
11:            $\theta_j = 90°$.
12:         **end if**
13:         **if** $\theta_j \leq \theta_{min}$ **then**
14:            $v_{min} = v_j$.
15:            $\theta_{min} = \theta_j$.
16:         **end if**
17:       **end for**
18:       Forward the packet to node v_{min}.
19:    **end if**
20: **end if**
21: **return** v_{min}

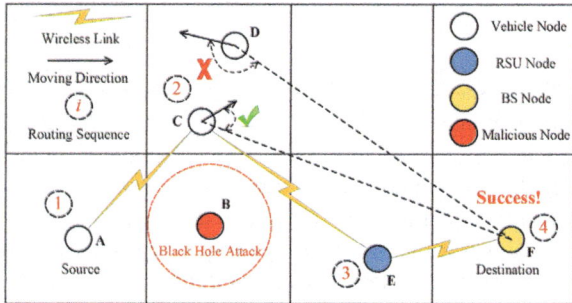

Fig. 5.3 Illustrative case of packet forwarding under the Grid-eJAL framework

node based on angular similarity, the computational cost per invocation is linear with respect to the number of candidate nodes, i.e., $O(q)$.

5.4 Performance Evaluation and Analysis

To assess the performance of the Grid-eJAL algorithm, we conduct simulation-based experiments. To emulate a realistic vehicular environment, we utilize the OpenStreetMap (OSM) editing tool [40] to manually extract a segment of the Washington DC map, which serves as our experimental topology. The chosen area spans $700 \times 700 \, m^2$ and is partitioned into a 10×10 grid. This urban layout contains

Table 5.1 Simulation parameters

Parameter	Value or range
Constant ξ	20
Discounted factor γ	0.5
Constant δ	0.995
Experimental area	$700 \times 700\,\text{m}^2$
Packet generating rate	60/second
Transmission range of vehicles	150 m
Transmission range of RSUs	200 m
Transmission range of BSs	600 m
Grid length	70 m
Time slot ΔT	1 s
TTL	10
Number of vehicles N	100
Number of RSUs L	100
Number of BS M	1
Number of malicious RSUs	8
Velocity of vehicles	$[0, 20]$ m/s
Packet drop probability $\mathcal{P}_d$	80%, 100%
Max Queue Length	500
Constant C^+	1500
Constant C^-	-30
Coefficient σ_i ($1 \leq i \leq N$)	1

208 intersections and 505 road segments. The simulations are performed using two complementary platforms: SUMO [41] and NS-3 [42]. SUMO is responsible for generating vehicular mobility traces on the extracted road map. In each run, N vehicles are randomly deployed, with initial locations and destinations assigned uniformly at random. The vehicle movement follows the Manhattan mobility model, incorporating both velocity constraints and probabilistic turning behavior at intersections. The generated mobility traces are then fed into NS-3, which is used to simulate the network communication environment. Each vehicle is equipped with two communication interfaces: IEEE 802.11p for V2V communication and LTE for V2I interactions. In the grid-based topology, RSUs are deployed at each intersection, and a BS, acting as the central destination node, is positioned at the center of the road map. This setup provides a representative testbed for evaluating communication and routing strategies in urban VANET scenarios. Table 5.1 lists the major simulation parameters used in the experiments. All reported performance metrics are averaged over 10 independent simulation runs, and standard errors are represented as error bars in the corresponding figures.

As Grid-eJAL is the first approach to integrate MARL with RM for enhancing attack resilience, we conduct comparative evaluations against several representative baseline algorithms:

5.4 Performance Evaluation and Analysis

- GPSR [43]: A position-based routing protocol that selects the neighboring node geographically closest to the destination.
- QGrid [20]: A Q-learning-based grid routing scheme that focuses on reducing communication overhead by selecting a relay node within the designated grid region.
- SEES [6]: A probabilistic multi-path routing strategy designed to ensure secure transmission and distribute forwarding load among intermediate nodes.
- CSR [44]: A trust-aware routing protocol that dynamically avoids malicious nodes by maximizing the overall trust score of the selected path.

5.4.1 Defense Performance

The attack success ratio serves as a primary indicator for evaluating the defense capability of routing algorithms. It is defined as the fraction of packets that are successfully dropped by adversaries out of the total number of packets generated. To rigorously assess the robustness of the proposed Grid-eJAL framework, we consider two adversarial scenarios, characterized by packet drop probabilities of $\mathcal{P}_d = 60\%$ and $\mathcal{P}_d = 100\%$, respectively. For each scenario, we simulate 300 epochs and compute the corresponding attack success ratios across Grid-eJAL and baseline algorithms.

As illustrated in Fig. 5.4a, the attack success ratio of Grid-eJAL rapidly converges to 1.5%, achieving the lowest value among all five evaluated algorithms. This indicates that Grid-eJAL provides superior adaptability and resilience against adversarial packet dropping. In comparison, the ratios of GPSR, SEES, and CSR remain relatively unchanged over time, suggesting limited responsiveness to dynamic attack strategies. QGrid, while not explicitly designed with security in mind, shows a noticeable decline in attack success ratio during the early episodes before stabilizing at a level comparable to that of SEES. This behavior likely stems from its Q-learning mechanism, which enables it to partially learn and circumvent packet losses induced by BHA and GHA attacks. Among all schemes, GPSR performs the worst in terms of defense, as it relies purely on geographic proximity for routing and lacks any mechanism to counter malicious behavior. SEES, on the other hand, benefits from its stochastic multi-path routing design, which improves robustness and reduces the attack success ratio to approximately 4.5%, outperforming GPSR by leveraging route diversity to mitigate the impact of adversaries.

The results shown in Fig. 5.4b provide further evidence of Grid-eJAL's superior defense performance. Specifically, its attack success ratio steadily declines from an initial value of 5% to approximately 1% as the learning process progresses. In contrast, QGrid begins at around 6% and gradually converges to a stable level near 4%. SEES demonstrates relatively consistent performance, with its attack success ratio remaining close to 4% throughout the evaluation. GPSR, lacking any learning or security-aware mechanism, exhibits the highest vulnerability, maintaining an attack success ratio of roughly 6% over all episodes.

Fig. 5.4 Comparison of five routing algorithms. (**a**) Drop probability $\mathcal{P}_d = 60\%$. (**b**) Drop probability $\mathcal{P}_d = 100\%$. (**a**) Attack success ratio comparison. (**b**) Attack success ratio comparison

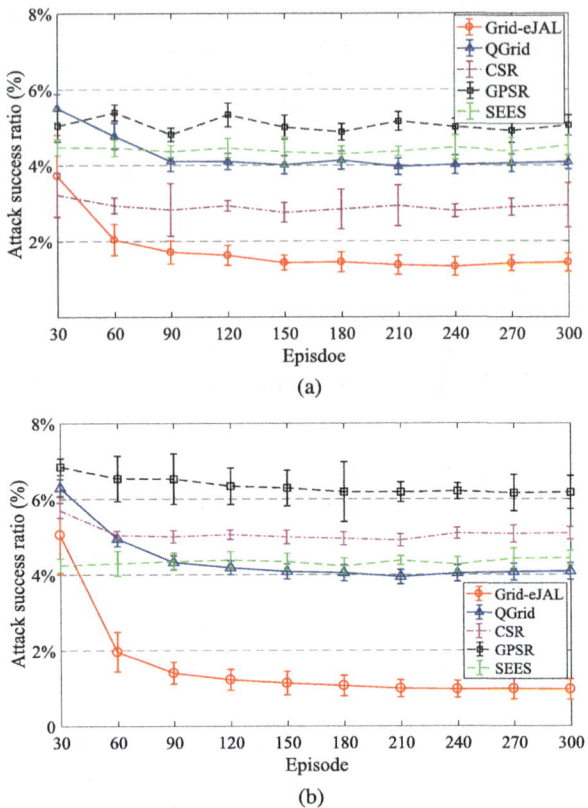

5.4.2 Network Performance

To comprehensively evaluate system effectiveness, we consider three fundamental indicators: packet delivery efficiency, transmission delay, and resource usage. Specifically, packet delivery efficiency refers to the proportion of data packets that successfully arrive at their intended destination relative to the total number of packets generated throughout the simulation period. The delay metric represents the average time required for a packet to reach the destination. For tractability, we adopt a common simplification used in prior studies [11, 12], assuming that the end-to-end delay is directly proportional to the number of hops, under the assumption of a homogeneous network environment. For resource consumption, our focus is on two components: computational energy and transmission energy. Based on prior works [45–47], the total energy expenditure from source to destination scales with both the hop count and the associated communication latency. Using these metrics, we compare the performance of Grid-eJAL against the baseline algorithms by analyzing the average delivery ratios and average hop counts over 300 simulation episodes.

5.4 Performance Evaluation and Analysis

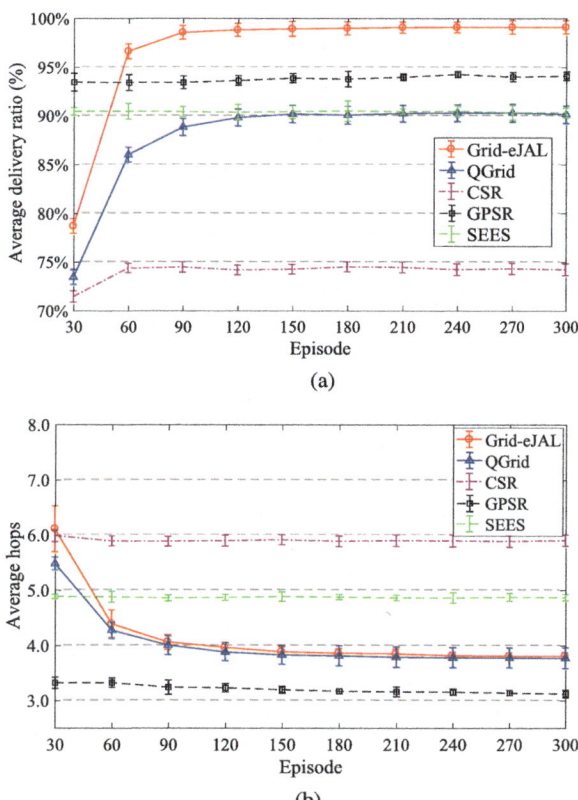

Fig. 5.5 Performance comparison of five routing algorithms over 300 episodes. (**a**) Average delivery ratio comparison with drop probability $\mathcal{P}_d = 100\%$. (**b**) Average hops comparison with drop probability $\mathcal{P}_d = 100\%$

The results in Fig. 5.5a shows that the average delivery ratios of the two learning-based approaches, Grid-eJAL and QGrid, exhibit an upward trend before convergence, whereas the ratios for the remaining algorithms remain largely unchanged throughout the simulation. Grid-eJAL shows a significant improvement in delivery ratio, rising from 80% to 99%, which highlights its ability to adaptively avoid malicious nodes and mitigate packet timeouts through reinforcement learning. QGrid also demonstrates performance gains, although to a lesser extent. Since it lacks explicit security mechanisms, it remains more vulnerable to adversarial behavior. As a result, despite Grid-eJAL operating in a distributed manner, it ultimately achieves a higher steady-state delivery ratio than QGrid. In contrast, CSR yields a comparatively lower delivery ratio. Although it incorporates trust-based security, the strict avoidance of potentially risky paths can lead to frequent delivery delays and timeouts, which negatively impact its overall effectiveness.

As shown in Fig. 5.5b, GPSR achieves the lowest average hop count among all evaluated algorithms, owing to its reliance on pure geographic proximity for routing. This outcome indicates that GPSR tends to reach the destination in fewer hops, suggesting relatively faster transmission—though at the cost of security. Both Grid-eJAL and QGrid exhibit a gradual decline in average hop count as learning

Fig. 5.6 Performance comparison of five routing algorithms in a scaled-up 1.4 km × 1.4 km network divided into 20 × 20 grids. (**a**) Average delivery ratio comparison with drop probability $\mathcal{P}_d = 100\%$. (**b**) Average hops comparison with drop probability $\mathcal{P}_d = 100\%$

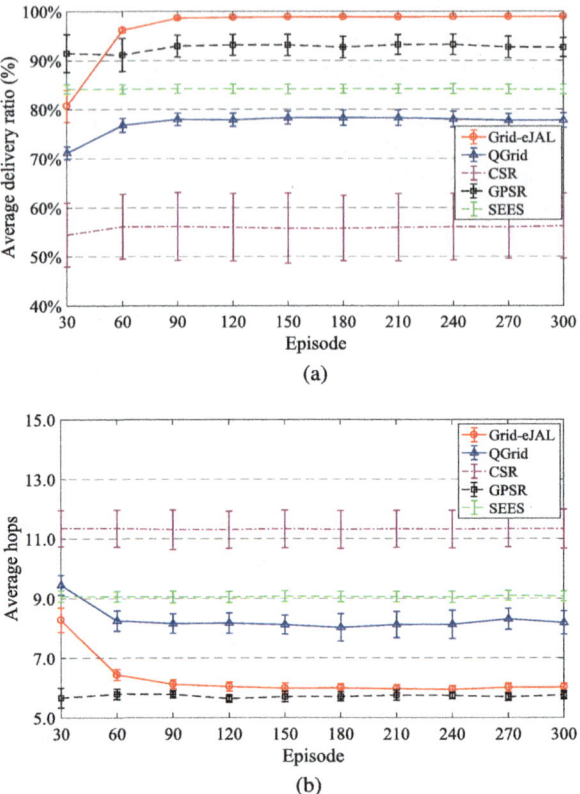

progresses, eventually stabilizing at approximately 4 hops. This demonstrates the ability to improve routing efficiency over time through adaptive learning. In contrast, SEES and CSR incur higher average hop counts, primarily because the design does not explicitly optimize for network efficiency or latency. SEES prioritizes route diversity, while CSR emphasizes trustworthiness, both of which may result in longer routing paths. These results collectively indicate that Grid-eJAL not only achieves superior delivery performance but also maintains a delay level comparable to that of non-secure learning-based alternatives. Moreover, when compared to security-centric algorithms, Grid-eJAL demonstrates more efficient resource utilization, offering a favorable trade-off between robustness and performance.

Next, we evaluate the scalability of the proposed approach by enlarging the simulation area to 1.4 km × 1.4 km, which is partitioned into a 20 × 20 grid. In this setting, the number of malicious RSUs is set to 16. We then compute the average delivery ratios and hop counts over 300 episodes. Compared with the results in Fig. 5.5a, the results presented in Fig. 5.6a indicate a noticeable decline in delivery ratio across all baseline algorithms, except Grid-eJAL. Notably, Grid-eJAL preserves a near-constant delivery ratio despite the expanded area and increased adversarial presence. Among the baseline methods, CSR exhibits the most pronounced drop, approximately 20%, highlighting its vulnerability under denser and more hostile network conditions. Additionally, results in Fig. 5.6b shows that the average hop count increases for all algorithms, suggesting elevated levels of latency and resource usage as the network scales. This trend is consistent with the increased geographic distance and communication complexity inherent in a larger area. Overall, these results confirm that Grid-eJAL maintains its superiority in terms of delivery ratio, delay, and resource consumption, even as the operating environment becomes more challenging.

5.5 Conclusion

Ensuring secure routing and reliable packet forwarding in VANETs remains a critical challenge due to their inherently dynamic nature and the vulnerability to various attacks, such as packet drop attacks. To address these issues, we propose Grid-eJAL, a hierarchical routing framework that combines MARL with RM to improve defense robustness. The proposed approach begins by dividing the physical environment into uniform grids, with the grid size aligned to the communication range of the vehicles. An adaptive online mechanism is then employed to select secure neighbor grids, wherein vehicles exchange jointly estimated Q-values with nearby agents to inform routing decisions. To further improve reliability, we introduce a minimum-angle selection strategy that identifies the most suitable relay node within the selected grid. Theoretical analysis confirms the convergence of the Grid-eJAL algorithm. Extensive simulation results validate its effectiveness in terms of delivery performance, latency, and resilience against attacks.

In future work, we plan to explore three key enhancements. First, we will examine the signaling overhead and the impact of GPS inaccuracies, both of which may affect performance in practical deployments. Second, we aim to integrate deep reinforcement learning techniques to extend Grid-eJAL into a Deep MARL framework. Additionally, by leveraging neural networks to approximate Q-functions, we will improve scalability and the potential to eliminate the need for predefined grid partitioning altogether.

References

1. Chbib, F., Khoukhi, L., Fahs, W., Haydar, J., Khatoun, R.: A cross-layered scheme for multichannel and reactive routing in vehicular ad hoc networks. Trans. Emerg. Telecommun. Technol. **33**(7), e4468 (2022)
2. Fadda, M., Murroni, M., Popescu, V.: Interference issues for vanet communications in the tvws in urban environments. IEEE Trans. Veh. Technol. **65**(7), 4952–4958 (2015)
3. Yamini, K.A.P., Stephy, J., Suthendran, K., Ravi, V.: Improving routing disruption attack detection in manets using efficient trust establishment. Trans. Emerg. Telecommun. Technol. **33**(5), e4446 (2022)

4. Sakai, K., Sun, M.-T., Ku, W.-S., Wu, J., Lai, T.H.: Secure data communications in wireless networks using multi-path avoidance routing. IEEE Trans. Wirel. Commun. **18**(10), 4753–4767 (2019)
5. Xiong, F., Li, A., Wang, H., Tang, L.: An sdn-mqtt based communication system for battlefield uav swarms. IEEE Commun. Mag. **57**(8), 41–47 (2019)
6. Sarkar, S., Datta, R.: A secure and energy-efficient stochastic multipath routing for self-organized mobile ad hoc networks. Ad Hoc Netw. **37**, 209–227 (2016)
7. Xia, H., Zhang, S.-s., Li, Y., Pan, Z.-k., Peng, X., Cheng, X.-z.: An attack-resistant trust inference model for securing routing in vehicular ad hoc networks. IEEE Trans. Veh. Technol. **68**(7), 7108–7120 (2019)
8. Rostamzadeh, K., Nicanfar, H., Torabi, N., Gopalakrishnan, S., Leung, V.C.M.: A context-aware trust-based information dissemination framework for vehicular networks. IEEE Internet Things J. **2**(2), 121–132 (2015)
9. Liu, Y., Dong, M., Ota, K., Liu, A.: Activetrust: secure and trustable routing in wireless sensor networks. IEEE Trans. Inf. Forensics Secur. **11**(9), 2013–2027 (2016)
10. Duan, Q., Al-Shaer, E., Jafarian, H.: Efficient random route mutation considering flow and network constraints. In: 2013 IEEE Conference on Communications and Network Security (CNS), pp. 260–268. IEEE (2013)
11. Gillani, F., Al-Shaer, E., Lo, S., Duan, Q., Ammar, M., Zegura, E.: Agile virtualized infrastructure to proactively defend against cyber attacks. In: 2015 IEEE Conference on Computer Communications (INFOCOM), pp. 729–737. IEEE (2015)
12. Zhang, H.-q., Lei, C., Chang, D.-x., Yang, Y.-j.: Network moving target defense technique based on collaborative mutation. Comput. Secur. **70**, 51–71 (2017)
13. Duan, Q., Al-Shaer, E., Chatterjee, S., Halappanavar, M., Oehmen, C.: Proactive routing mutation against stealthy distributed denial of service attacks: metrics, modeling, and analysis. J. Def. Model. Simul. **15**(2), 219–230 (2018)
14. Zhang, T., Kuang, X., Zhou, Z., Gao, H., Xu, C.: An intelligent route mutation mechanism against mixed attack based on security awareness. In: 2019 IEEE Global Communications Conference (GLOBECOM), pp. 1–6. IEEE (2019)
15. Xu, C., Zhang, T., Kuang, X., Zhou, Z., Yu, S.: Context-aware adaptive route mutation scheme: a reinforcement learning approach. IEEE Internet Things J. **8**(17), 13528–13541 (2021)
16. Kang, M.S., Lee, S.B., Gligor, V.D.: The crossfire attack. In: 2013 IEEE Symposium on Security and Privacy, pp. 127–141. IEEE (2013)
17. Hurtado, L.A., Mocanu, E., Nguyen, P.H., Gibescu, M., Kamphuis, R.I.G.: Enabling cooperative behavior for building demand response based on extended joint action learning. IEEE Trans. Ind. Inform. **14**(1), 127–136 (2017)
18. Zhang, K., Yang, Z., Liu, H., Zhang, T., Basar, T.: Fully decentralized multi-agent reinforcement learning with networked agents. In: International Conference on Machine Learning, pp. 5872–5881. PMLR (2018)
19. Zhang, T., Xu, C., Zou, P., Tian, H., Kuang, X., Yang, S., Zhong, L., Niyato, D.: How to mitigate ddos intelligently in sd-iov: a moving target defense approach. IEEE Trans. Ind. Inform. **19**(1), 1097–1106 (2022)
20. Li, F., Song, X., Chen, H., Li, X., Wang, Y.: Hierarchical routing for vehicular ad hoc networks via reinforcement learning. IEEE Trans. Veh. Technol. **68**(2), 1852–1865 (2018)
21. Luo, L., Sheng, L., Yu, H., Sun, G.: Intersection-based v2x routing via reinforcement learning in vehicular ad hoc networks. IEEE Trans. Intell. Transp. Syst. **23**(6), 5446–5459 (2021)
22. Zhang, D., Yu, F.R., Yang, R., Zhu, L.: Software-defined vehicular networks with trust management: a deep reinforcement learning approach. IEEE Trans. Intell. Transp. Syst. **23**(2), 1400–1414 (2020)
23. Cui, J., Liu, Y., Nallanathan, A.: Multi-agent reinforcement learning-based resource allocation for uav networks. IEEE Trans. Wirel. Commun. **19**(2), 729–743 (2019)
24. Peng, H., Shen, X.: Multi-agent reinforcement learning based resource management in mec- and uav-assisted vehicular networks. IEEE J. Sel. Areas Commun. **39**(1), 131–141 (2020)
25. Bai, F., Sadagopan, N., Helmy, A.: The important framework for analyzing the impact of mobility on performance of routing protocols for adhoc networks. Ad Hoc Netw. **1**(4), 383–403 (2003)

26. Li, C., Fu, Y., Yu, F.R., Luan, T.H., Zhang, Y.: Vehicle position correction: a vehicular blockchain networks-based gps error sharing framework. IEEE Trans. Intell. Transp. Syst. **22**(2), 898–912 (2020)
27. Demetriou, S., Jain, P., Kim, K.-H.: Codrive: improving automobile positioning via collaborative driving. In: IEEE INFOCOM 2018-IEEE Conference on Computer Communications, pp. 72–80. IEEE (2018)
28. Qin, H., Peng, Y., Zhang, W.: Vehicles on rfid: error-cognitive vehicle localization in gps-less environments. IEEE Trans. Veh. Technol. **66**(11), 9943–9957 (2017)
29. Jo, K., Chu, K., Sunwoo, M.: Interacting multiple model filter-based sensor fusion of gps with in-vehicle sensors for real-time vehicle positioning. IEEE Trans. Intell. Transp. Syst. **13**(1), 329–343 (2011)
30. Shu, T., Krunz, M., Liu, S.: Secure data collection in wireless sensor networks using randomized dispersive routes. IEEE Trans. Mob. Comput. **9**(7), 941–954 (2010)
31. Duan, Q., Al-Shaer, E., Xie, J.: Range and topology mutation based wireless agility. In: Proceedings of the 7th ACM Workshop on Moving Target Defense, pp. 59–67 (2020)
32. Schweitzer, N., Stulman, A., Margalit, R.D., Shabtai, A.: Contradiction based gray-hole attack minimization for ad-hoc networks. IEEE Trans. Mob. Comput. **16**(8), 2174–2183 (2016)
33. Jiang, W., Feng, G., Qin, S., Shing Peter Yum, T., Cao, G.: Multi-agent reinforcement learning for efficient content caching in mobile d2d networks. IEEE Trans. Wirel. Commun. **18**(3), 1610–1622 (2019)
34. He, T., Bao, J., Li, R., Ruan, S., Li, Y., Song, L., He, H., Zheng, Y.: What is the human mobility in a new city: transfer mobility knowledge across cities. In: Proceedings of the Web Conference 2020, pp. 1355–1365 (2020)
35. Yao, F., Jia, L.: A collaborative multi-agent reinforcement learning anti-jamming algorithm in wireless networks. IEEE Wirel. Commun. Lett. **8**(4), 1024–1027 (2019)
36. Yan, Y., Zhang, B., Li, C., Su, C.: Cooperative caching and fetching in d2d communications-a fully decentralized multi-agent reinforcement learning approach. IEEE Trans. Veh. Technol. **69**(12), 16095–16109 (2020)
37. Jiang, W., Feng, G., Qin, S., Shing Peter Yum, T., Cao,G.: Multi-agent reinforcement learning for efficient content caching in mobile d2d networks. IEEE Trans. Wirel. Commun. **18**(3), 1610–1622 (2019)
38. Kim, D., Moon, S., Hostallero, D., Kang, W.J., Lee, T., Son, K., Yi, Y.: Learning to schedule communication in multi-agent reinforcement learning (2019). arXiv preprint arXiv:1902.01554
39. Feng, J., Li, H., Huang, M., Liu, S., Ou, W., Wang, Z., Zhu, X.: Learning to collaborate: multi-scenario ranking via multi-agent reinforcement learning. In: Proceedings of the 2018 World Wide Web Conference, pp. 1939–1948 (2018)
40. Haklay, M., Weber, P.: Openstreetmap: user-generated street maps. IEEE Pervasive Comput. **7**(4), 12–18 (2008)
41. The simulation of urban mobility. http://sumo.sourceforge.net. Accessed 13 December 2020
42. The ns-3 network simulator. https://www.nsnam.org. Accessed 4 March 2022
43. Karp., B., Kung, H.-T.: Gpsr: greedy perimeter stateless routing for wireless networks. In: Proceedings of the 6th Annual International Conference on Mobile Computing and Networking, pp. 243–254 (2000)
44. Yun, J., Seo, S., Chung, J.-M.: Centralized trust-based secure routing in wireless networks. IEEE Wirel. Commun. Lett. **7**(6), 1066–1069 (2018)
45. Wu, Y., Wu, J., Chen, L., Yan, J., Han, Y.: Load balance guaranteed vehicle-to-vehicle computation offloading for min-max fairness in vanets. IEEE Trans. Intell. Transp. Syst. **23**(8), 11994–12013 (2021)
46. Yang, Y., Zhao, S., Zhang, W., Chen, Y., Luo, X., Wang, J.: Debts: delay energy balanced task scheduling in homogeneous fog networks. IEEE Internet Things J. **5**(3), 2094–2106 (2018)
47. Dinh, T.Q., Tang, J., La, Q.D., Quek, T.Q.S.: Offloading in mobile edge computing: task allocation and computational frequency scaling. IEEE Trans. Commun. **65**(8), 3571–3584 (2017)

Chapter 6
Conclusion

Abstract In this chapter, we will summarize this book and discuss potential future directions for MTD.

Keywords Moving target defense · Artificial intelligence · Cloud-edge-terminal network

6.1 Summary of the Book

Cloud-edge-terminal network architecture has emerged as a crucial piece of infrastructure in the contemporary digital era, supporting a wide range of application scenarios. Through the cooperation of cloud computing, edge computing, and terminal devices, this network architecture offers consumers scalable, low-latency, and effective services. However, as cloud-edge-terminal networks are widely used, their security issues are becoming increasingly apparent. Since this architecture involves the collaboration of multiple layers and nodes, attackers are able to utilize its complexity and openness to launch multiple forms of attacks, such as data loss attacks, Distributed Denial of Service attack (DDoS) attacks, and man-in-the-middle attacks.

Currently, moving target defense (MTD) is a successful strategy for addressing the growing security threats to cloud-edge-terminal networks. By dynamically altering the system's attack surface, MTD strengthens network security by making it harder for attackers to identify the system's vulnerabilities. However, traditional MTD schemes still face some challenges under the cloud-edge-terminal network architecture: (1) inability to adapt, which makes it likely to perform poorly in the face of sophisticated assaults; (2) insufficient intelligence in defense strategies; (3) insufficient consideration of network communication situations while defending; (4) lack of a unified coordinating mechanism for multiple MTD schemes to be deployed in concert.

To address the above problems, we try to introduce AI techniques into MTD to enhance its adaptability and defense capability. In this book, we propose intelligent

MTD solutions for a variety of cloud-side-terminal network scenarios, providing targeted security protection strategies for different application scenarios:

1. **Host Address Mutation Based on Advantage Actor-Critic Approach.** To defend against network reconnaissance attacks, we propose Intelligence-Driven Host Address Mutation (ID-HAM), which is a Host Address Mutation (HAM) based on advantage actor-critic algorithm. In order to characterize the network circumstances, we first create a Markov Decision Process (MDP). In particular, we set the network state to the host type, the action to the host-to-host assignment shuffle, and the state transfer to the change in the number of hosts IP address changes. The address-to-host assignment issue is therefore formulated as a constraint fulfillment problem, where we take into account limitations such as flow table widths, banned blocks, and mutation rates. By solving this problem, we can remove infeasible actions from the MDP's action space. Finally, based on our previously defined MDP, we design an advantaged actor-critic algorithm. This algorithm enables the reorganization of the address-host assignment relationship, and then periodically selects mutating IP addresses to associate with hosts based on different mutation rates. Our proposed MTD scheme can learn from scanning behavior to improve the defense performance. Through security analysis and Mininet simulation studies, we verify the efficacy of our approach.
2. **Collaborative Mutation-Based Moving Target Defense Based on Hierarchical Reinforcement Learning.** We design CM-MTD, a cooperative mutation-based MTD, in Digital Twins Mobile Networks (DTMNs). First, we use a Semi-Markov Decision Process (SMDP) to describe time-varying security incidents and the dynamic implementation of multi-MTD schemes. We set the network state as the joint prediction result of security events for all network nodes, and set the macro-action as selecting a deployment policy, the action as deployment policy selection, and the base action as executing a specific MTD scheme deployment. Then, We use Long Short-Term Memory (LSTM) to forecast future security events that provide inputs to the network state. We also model IP address space allocation and routing variant selection as constraint satisfaction problems according to Satisfiability Modeling Theory (SMT) and consider practical constraints such as flow table size, operation cost and quality of service. By dealing with this problem, inactionable actions are removed from the action space.
3. **Roadside Unit Mutation via Proximal Policy Optimization.** We create a clever DRL-based MTD method to protect Software Defined Internet of Vehicles (SD-IoV) against DDoS assaults. We take the topic of determining the best configuration for roadside units (RSUs) as an optimization issue that is tackled using DRL after modeling the mutation of network configurations as MDPs. To identify normal and spy vehicles in the network, We create a method for assessing confidence in RSU-vehicle associations. In the dynamic adjustment process, we formalize the network constraints using SMT. We conducted simulation experiments on our scheme using the network simulator NS-3, and the results show that our approach performs better than current representative systems.

4. **Route Mutation via Multiagent Reinforcement Learning.** We design an intelligent RM scheme for defense against packet drop attacks in Vehicular Ad hoc Networks (VANETs). We start by dividing the region into uniformly sized grids. Next, we convert the vehicle's forwarding process formula into an MDP, where the network state is set to the grid where it is currently located, the destination grid where the packet is transmitted, and the time-to-live (TTL) value of the packet that is about to be forwarded, and the vehicle action is set to the selection of a safe neighboring grid. Subsequently, we design an online adaptive multi-agent reinforcement learning (MARL) for allowing the agent to select a safe neighbor grid. In our approach, agents can share their parameters to achieve adaptive and faster convergence of Q-values, estimation of state-action pairs. We use a self-designed minimum angle selection strategy for finding the relay node in the grid that determines the highest probability of successfully transmitting a packet after selecting the next-hop grid. We have verified through simulation experiments that our proposed intelligent RM scheme has a success rate of more than 99% in defending against packet drop attacks.

6.2 Future Directions

MTD has shown good defense performance in many complex network environments, but with the development of network technology and the increasingly serious security situation, MTD must keep pace with the times and further improve its scalability, adaptability and defense capabilities.

1. **Network Scenario Adaptation and Extension for Intelligent MTDs.** The application of intelligent MTD solutions to broader networking scenarios, such as software-defined wide area networks (SD-WAN) and distributed SDN, is an important future research direction. In the face of network architectures with varying characteristics, this inevitably poses some unique challenges during deployment. For example, how to ensure seamless transmission of packets with virtual IP (vIP) addresses across multiple domains in SD-WAN, and how MTDs can be quickly adapted to dynamic network topology changes in distributed SDN scenarios. To this aim, exploring generalized design frameworks and efficient adaptation mechanisms will be key to driving the scalability of intelligent MTD solutions.
2. **Enhancing the Adaptive Capability of Intelligent MTD Programs.** Adaptation to emerging network conditions and new environments is a key performance metric for intelligent MTD solutions. In the increasingly complex network environments of the future, only by enhancing the adaptive capability of MTD schemes can ensure that they are fully effective in various scenarios. For example, in the future, we plan to improve the adaptability of our proposed ID-HAM by optimizing the state-space modeling and introducing the SMT solving mechanism to effectively eliminate actions that are not suitable for the current

network environment. And, to enhance the adaptive capability of the CM-MTD, we will also focus on the optimization of the incentive design to accelerate up the convergence of the model so that it can quickly adapt to the dynamically changing environment. The continuous exploration of these research directions will provide greater flexibility and higher adaptive efficiency for future MTD solutions.

3. **Introduction of Advanced AI Technology.** In the face of various challenges that may arise in the future application and deployment of intelligent MTD schemes, it would be an effective approach to try to introduce advanced AI techniques for solving these problems. For example, the complexity of large-scale state and action spaces can be effectively dealt with by DRL and deep MARL techniques, thus improving the decision-making efficiency and robustness of the scheme. The combination of these techniques will provide MTD schemes with enhanced intelligence capabilities to cope with complex and changing network environments.

Made in the USA
Monee, IL
03 May 2026